LIKE FIRE IN HIS VEINS

LIKE FIRE IN HIS VEINS

GOLDIE M. DOWN

Review and Herald Publishing Association
Washington, D.C.

This book was
Edited by Gerald Wheeler
Designed by Robert Wright
Cover Illustration by Bobbi Tull

Type set: 10 on 11 by 21 Bask

Printed in U.S.A.

Library of Congress Cataloging in Publication Data
Down, Goldie M.
    Like fire in his veins.
    1. Crabtree, Abe. 2. Crabtree, Tom. 3. Crabtree, David.
4. Seventh-day Adventists—Australia—New South Wales—Biogra-
phy. 5. New South Wales—Biography.
I. Title.
BX6191.D68   286.7'3 [B]   81-23339
ISBN 0-8280-0104-9   AACR2

DEDICATION

This book is dedicated to Tom and Rosie,
to my parents Herbert and Violet Scarr,
and to all the other men and women who
pioneered the third angel's message in
the dairying and banana-growing country
of New South Wales' far north coast.

CONTENTS

MURDER IN THE
GOLDFIELDS

Kill them rabbits, you kids! Get rid of them!" Old man
Crabtree's walrus mustache quivered with rage as he
shook his fist at the retreating children. "There's too many
rabbits chewing up the grass, taking all the graziers' profits. Get
rid of them, I say!"

As soon as he was a safe distance from his grandfather,
6-year-old Tom stopped and cradled the furry bundle in his
hands. "Don't be afraid, little bunny," he crooned. "I won't let
grandpa hurt you."

Still keeping a wary eye on the irate old man hobbling up
the hill after them, the three brothers backed into the kitchen to
the protection afforded by their mother's domain. Since
grandma's death, she was the only one who could handle the
old man's rages.

"Hush," she said when he thundered up to the door and the
air around him turned blue with his curses. "Hush, Grandpa.
Not in front of the children."

The old man's turkey-red cheeks flamed even brighter and
the veins in his neck stood out like ropes as he struggled to
choke back his oaths. His fierce blue eyes sparked and his
mustache jerked as violently as his sinewy arms. For long
minutes he glared at the children cowering behind their
mother's skirt, daring them to disobey his orders. Then he
turned on his heel and limped off, the three-inch sole on his
right boot clomping noisily over the hard-packed earth.

Grandpa Crabtree had not always been crippled and
crochety. When, as Abraham Crabbtyre, he sailed away from
England during the middle years of the nineteenth century, his
shock of brown hair had been neatly combed and his keen

blue eyes shone with eagerness for adventure.

A scion of the noble family of Crabbtyre, who traced their ancestry directly back to A.D. 1301, when the king of England granted them a coat of arms featuring a grasped dagger and the motto "In God is my trust," Abraham set less store in God than in the fact that a brawny hand held the knife. He always carried a gun and a wicked-looking dagger, and his interpretation of the family motto could well have been, "All right, trust God if you like, but do what you can to help yourself."

The details of Abraham Crabbtyre's early life and who or what he left behind in England have gone to the grave with him. But he was about 37 years old and an experienced seaman when his ship set off for Australia around 1855.

Fifty years earlier convicts had crowded the sailing ships bound for the newly settled colony. After the Revolutionary War, Britain could no longer send her unwanted felons to America, so men and women culled from England's noisome, overcrowded jails—some of them imprisoned for crimes as small as stealing a loaf of bread or riding on a horse without asking the owner's permission—found themselves transported to the new land.

But now the stately masted ships bulged with free settlers coming out to make their fortunes. News of rich farming and grazing lands easily acquired, of fortunes earned through trading and manufacturing, and recently of the gold that had been discovered sent men and women streaming from the British Isles.

During the long voyage to Australia the emigrants talked of little else than the money they planned to make in the new colony. Gold had been discovered in New South Wales and Victoria. Men's eyes lighted up at the thought of the wealth that was theirs for the finding.

Words such as *cradling, panning, dirt,* and *color* permeated every conversation. Every person aboard, down to the smallest child, had definite ideas of what he would do if he struck it rich.

The ship's crew also caught the fever. Even a salty-blooded sailor like Abe, with the smell of sea spray in his nostrils and the roar of wind and waves thundering in his ears, could not resist the lure of gold. "Keep your ears open and learn all you can before we get there." He winked and nodded a knowing head at his fellow crew members.

They grinned and heeded his advice. While they tended rigging and mended sails, swabbed the decks or tarred the ropes, they kept one eye on the emigrants and one ear tuned to their conversations.

"As soon as you disembark at Melbourne you make straight for the goldfields," a well-informed man with pale eyes and sandy side whiskers told the crowd of fortune seekers hanging on to his every word. "My brother has been in Victoria for a couple of years, and he wrote me what to do." He cleared his throat and leaned over the ship's rail to spit, slowly and deliberately, into the churning sea. "Don't waste any time," he said. "You might miss out on some nuggets, them big lumps of gold lying around on top of the ground. Get your gear and make straight for Ballarat."

"I've got an uncle that's a coal miner in Wales." One of the crowd braced his body against the ship's roll and stood up to have his say. "He told me that once yer get the surface stuff out, yer gotta go deep. The system's much the same fer coal or fer gold, he said."

"No," Sandy Whiskers disagreed. "Gold's easier. But you must get your gear first."

Gear, Abe and the other sailors learned by listening, consisted of the pick and shovel one needed for digging out the gold-streaked gravel; pans and sieves for washing the dirt; and ropes, buckets, and windlass for when the hole grew too deep for surface scratching.

It sounded easy. The sailors talked it over among themselves and made their secret plans. As soon as the ship berthed in Melbourne port, Abe Crabtree (as he became known), along with the passengers—and most of the other sailors and crew—deserted his ship and set out on foot for the promised riches of the gold mines of Ballarat.

It did not turn out to be as easy as it sounded when discussed on the rolling deck of the sailing ship, with the cloudless azure sky above and the tossing indigo waves below and not a hint on the horizon of the arduous work that lay ahead.

Buying the necessary equipment and getting to Ballarat goldfield was an ordeal in itself.

As soon as the passengers and sailors stepped ashore greedy-eyed individuals willing to arrange transport, and to sell, at a price, the axes and shovels, buckets, ropes, and everything else needed to mine gold, accosted the eager would-be miners. Often the newcomers lacked enough money to purchase even the bare essentials. But that did not stop them. With the glint of gold in front of their eyes, they either went ahead and hoped for a miracle or bartered some of the treasured trifles that they had carried all the way from England. The few who could afford the fare traveled by coach or hired horses to carry their loads. But most walked the seventy miles with their blanket-rolled swags on their backs.

For thirty shillings Abe bought a license that gave him the right to dig for one month in an area eight feet square. It was his "claim," which he would protect with his life if need be. Since claims in and around the creek beds were the most sought after, latecomers like him had to be content with staking their pegs on nearby hills and digging deeper in search of color.

"What are you, an' where'd you come from?" The bearded man working the adjoining claim spat on his hands and rubbed them together before reaching for his pick.

"A sailor—from England."

"Huh," the man grunted. "They're all here—the butcher, the baker, the candlestick maker, an' doctors, lawyers, an' bobbies as well. Do you know"—he guffawed in midsentence—"do you know that one time there were only two policemen left in Melbourne? The rest of them had cleared out to the diggings."

He laughed again and plied his pick energetically for a few

minutes before he stopped to ask, " 'Ave you got a mate?"

"No, I plan to work by myself."

The bearded one shook his head. "It's better if two or three work together, 'specially when you gotta go deep. One can get down an' dig in the shaft, an' another on top can send down the rope an' bring up the buckets o' gravel. An' the tother one can do the washin'. My missus 'elps me." He nodded in the direction of a sun-bonneted figure at the foot of the hill. "She does the pannin'."

Before he bent to his task again, he fired another question. "Where're you livin'?"

"I only arrived here yesterday." Abe pointed to his swollen feet. "Last night I slept under the stars, but——"

"Looks like rain comin' up." He squinted at the sky and broke in on Abe's reply. "If you can't afford a tent, you'd better build a 'umpy."

"A humpy?"

The man grinned crookedly and leaned on his pick. "Looks as if you don't know nuthin'." Then he pointed to the jumble of tents and huts, barely discernible through the dust and campfire smoke. "They're 'umpies."

Abe gazed at the haphazard collection of canvas, stone, and timber, and his heart felt as heavy as an anchor. Where, in all the seething mass of humanity, could he hope to find a toehold? The whole area roiled like a stirred-up ants' nest. Men, women, and horses worked like slaves driven by an invisible master. Even small children scurried around picking up rocks, scrabbling in the dirt, wading into the stream to wash pans of gravel. He caught their excited cries above the splash of water and the dull thud of picks. Gold fever tingled in his veins. His heart pounded. If they could find gold, so could he.

In an amazingly short time he erected his own humpy. For walls he packed wet clay and gravel tightly between rough timber posts and topped them with a canvas roof. As he worked he noticed that some of the family men had built quite large huts of sun-dried bricks, with stone fireplaces and chimneys.

Abe shrugged. So long as it kept out the weather, his was good enough. He drove a couple of wooden pegs into the mud walls and hung up his spare shirt and trousers and his hurricane lamp.

Bearded Alf inspected the structure and showed him how to arrange three or four large stones to make an outside fireplace. "All you need now is some provisions and a couple o' buckets fer carryin' water." He nodded approvingly.

With a grin, Abe rattled the few coins left in his pocket. "Might as well get everything I need now," he said and trudged up the hill to the straggling main street, where the merchants, the tavern, the police, and the government had set up more or less permanent stone and timber buildings.

Soon he returned with a sack of flour and smaller quantities of tea, sugar, and salt, plus a pick, pannikin, and buckets, and a pouchful of tarry-black tobacco. It was quite a load, and Abe breathed heavily as he tossed his purchases onto the dirt floor of the humpy.

Now he was ready to dig. Almost trembling with eagerness, he chose a corner of his claim, raised his pick, and swung it down on the hard-baked earth. It took a long time and a lot of muscle to dig even a small hole, and certainly no nuggets popped out to meet him.

His back ached and his hands blistered, but he kept doggedly on. He'd paid for his claim, and he was going to keep at it until he got some returns.

Life soon settled into a monotonous routine. From sunup to sundown, Monday to Saturday, Abe worked like all the other gold-fevered prospectors—in a stifling haze of heat and red dust raised by thousands of shovels and pickaxes biting into the earth. The constant creak and clank of buckets and windlasses at the bigger mines and men shouting at their plodding workhorses barely penetrated his consciousness. His pink-and-white English skin burned to a freckled tan, and his muscles bulged and strengthened.

He made no spectacular finds.

"Only a few lucky blokes find nuggets," Alf said. The rest,

like he and Abe, toiled and sweated and swore their way through the sunbaked soil, month after month, for the occasional speck of gold that kept their hopes alive.

Eventually some of the men gave up and went back to the trades for which they had trained: carpenters, soapmakers, tinsmiths, and coopers. Others, considering a steady wage, however small, better than the unreliable riches of gold mining, straggled out to the country and worked for labor-hungry farmers and cattle owners.

But most of the gold seekers kept on mining. Lured by hopes of a big find, they trailed from one diggings to another. Always hoping to strike it rich tomorrow, they slept in crude huts and ate damper (bread made without yeast and baked in the ashes) and molasses, washed down with mugs of scalding billy tea. They dug from dawn till dusk in all kinds of weather. Although they developed rheumatism, chest problems, and sore eyes, they kept at it, their gambling instincts fired by an occasional gleam of gold in the dirt they so carefully panned.

By dint of constant toil Abe dug out enough gold to pay his way but never enough to make him rich. Sometimes he sighed and straightened his aching back, leaning on his pick handle while he shaded his eyes with a calloused hand and gazed away into the blue distance. Did he regret having left the sea? No one ever knew.

Tantalized by his hopes, Abe hung around the goldfields for nearly a decade. Several times during those years he threw down his pick in disgust and went to the bush to work on cattle stations or to pick up droving jobs. Riding with experienced men herding cattle down to the coast for shipment, Abe soon knew the country well. Two or three trips and he had friends in all the small towns between Ballarat and the South Australian border. His courtly English manners, brought out whenever he wanted to charm, made him a favorite with some as easily as his trigger temper made him an enemy with others.

"There's a big droving job going, if you're interested," Bullety Bob told him one day. "Me an' Shorty Mulligan an' some others are taking a mob down to the coast. Be away a couple of months. We'll be glad to have a good hand like you."

"Righto." Abe rolled up his swag, slammed the door of his hut, and tucked his revolver into its holster. "I'm ready."

"Thought you'd come." Bob grinned. "I got a good horse waiting for you. We'll meet Shorty and the bullock cart of supplies at the crossroads and pick up the herd from Mr. Millier's place tomorrow."

"Righto." Crabtree jammed his battered felt hat firmly in place, shouldered his swag, and accompanied Bob across the paddock to the waiting horses.

Abe and the other drovers found the first few days on the road quiet enough. The cattle, lazy and well-fed after weeks spent in the fattening paddocks, plodded amiably along, raising clouds of dust that shrouded the horsemen. At night the drovers built a huge campfire, and the cook boiled the billy* for tea and baked damper in the glowing coals. If the night was cold or wet, the men pitched tents, but in clear weather they rolled up in their swags beside the fire.

The drovers took turns at the night watch. The cattle, loosely bunched together, were unlikely to stray far from the watchful dogs, but the possibility always existed that something might frighten the unpredictable creatures and scatter the herd far and wide.

Abe's brain was as keen as his temper was quick. On the droving trips with the men who had tamed the grand new country, so different from their native England, he absorbed bushmanship like a sponge. He learned to handle horses and cattle, to kindle fire in the native way, to recognize signs of water where none seemed present. If it hadn't been for the gold fever burning in his veins, he might have been content to seek his fortune with the cattlemen. As it was, he considered the cattle drives as merely a holiday from digging.

At each stopping place the drovers set the hobbled bullocks loose to graze and propped the heavy cart with its load of supplies against a tree stump. After they'd eaten, the men lounged around the campfire, smoking and yarning, each one trying to outdo the other with the tallness of his tale or

---

* A metal can or other vessel with a lid.

the richness of his reminiscences.

Gradually the voices faded, pipes smoldered and went out, and one by one the men stretched out on the sun-hardened ground and slept. Only the quiet thud of hoofbeats and the occasional crack of a burning stick pierced the dark stillness.

One night—how or why no one ever knew—the heavy supply cart lost its precarious balance on the tree stump. The huge, iron-shod wheels made a turn or two before the cart's tongue dug into the earth and stopped its movement.

Only a turn or two, but far enough to crush a leg of the nearest sleeper. Abe woke with a yell of pain and surprise and found himself pinned under one of the wheels.

The other men jerked out of their sleep with shouts and curses. Dogs barked, and the patrolling horsemen galloped back to the camp. Somebody stirred up the fire, and by its flickering light Abe's mates strained to push the cart aside and drag him free.

"'Is leg's broke." Shorty Mulligan made an instant diagnosis and rummaged among their stores for the brandy bottle—the bushman's cure for all ills. He poured the groaning man a stiff dose.

"Here y' are. This'll ease yer pain, mate." He held the mug to Abe's lips while over his shoulders he issued instructions to the rest. "Find a straight sapling, Bob, and peel the bark clean off it. There's an old blanket under me 'orse's saddle, 'Arry. Tear it into strips an' we'll tie 'is leg up."

Abe bit his lips to hold back his groans as the men's clumsy hands lifted his injured leg. They lowered it into the natural curve of the treebark and then bound leg and splint together to keep them immobile.

His thigh had broken in two places. The droving party was too far along the way to think of going back, so for six long weeks Abe lay in the jolting provisions cart while his mates herded the cattle along the tedious trail.

By the time Shorty decided that the bone had knit and he could remove the splint, Abe's right leg was more than three inches shorter than his left. The broken ends of bone had healed together on top of each other. Shorty and his mates did not know that they should have stretched his leg out to position the bones before attaching the splint. Possibly if they had known, and had tried to do it, they would have done more damage than they did. At least that was how Abe comforted himself when he saw the results of Shorty's bush doctoring.

From that time on, despite the thick-soled leather boot that he eventually wore, Abe limped badly and earned the nickname Hopping Abe.

With further droving out of the question until his injured leg strengthened, Abe returned to Ballarat and a new claim.

For once fortune smiled upon his hard work. Slowly the store of gold dust he deposited in his miner's bank (the heavy cloth belt he wore around his waist under his clothes), grew into a sizable amount.

"Why don't yer put yer gold dust in the bank?" Old Alf, his back bent from countless hours of digging, his bushy beard grayer and more unkempt, was still Abe's closest friend.

"No, indeed." Like most miners, Abe distrusted the solitary bank that operated from a tent in the struggling settlement's main street. He jerked his head toward it and patted his waist meaningfully. "Better to take care of one's own interests."

"Yer takin' awful risks," Alf warned. "At least take it ter the gold office and have it weighed and sent orf ter Melbourne."

"No, sir! There are too many blankety-blank bushrangers* around. Likely I'd lose the lot."

Alf mumbled into his beard and went on chipping away at his claim. He knew Abe was right. Despite its armed escort, all too often robbers held up the mailcoach at gunpoint and robbed it of the gold it carried.

So it came about that Abraham Crabtree had twelve hundred sovereigns' worth of gold in his belt pockets the night he woke in his rough hut and felt the heavy bulk of someone straddling his body. Calloused fingers pressed into his windpipe. Instantly he knew that a thief was about to murder him for his gold.

Half-dazed with sleep and fear, he tried to wrestle his

---

* Bushrangers, an Australian term for armed outlaws who robbed banks and coaches.

attacker, but the cruel fingers dug deeper into his throat. Frantically, Abe wriggled and twisted one arm free of the pinioning knees and reached for the .44 lying at his side. The blood swelled and pounded in his brain. His eyes seemed about to pop from his bursting head. In a last desperate move his fingers closed around the trigger and he fired upward.

The shot reverberated like a thunderclap. Flashes of light stabbed through Abe's eyes and into his throbbing head. His whole body convulsed as the choking fingers slowly released their hold and the heavy bulk atop him tumbled onto the hard dirt floor.

For a few seconds Abe lay choking and gasping. Then, with the sound of the shot still in his ears, he snatched up his boots and ran. In a minute the whole camp would be astir. Men would mill about asking what the noise was, wondering what had happened. They'd rouse the police, the troopers. Already a tiny flicker of light away over on his left showed that someone had lighted a hurricane lantern. The search was on.

As swift and silent as a hare Abe ran, not knowing which way he was headed. He didn't care. Anywhere. Anywhere, as long as it was away from this accursed goldfield. Abe Crabtree had killed a man—he was a murderer. The troopers would be after him . . . hunting him down like an animal. If they caught him he'd hang. His breath sobbed in his bruised throat. Hang! He hadn't meant to kill—he'd only acted in self-defense.

Blindly he pushed on until dawn's pale light showed that he had fled west toward the South Australian border. Good. Abe had been that way before. He could walk two hundred miles . . . surely he could. If not, he knew a shepherd's hut . . . he would hide . . . until the hunt died down. How long would that be?

The sun peered above the horizon, and Abe plunged wearily off the dirt road into the thorny, clinging bush. After fighting his way through the tangled undergrowth, he climbed a leafy tree where he could be safe from snakes and ants. Wedging his body tightly into a forked branch, he dozed fitfully through the long daylight hours.

As soon as darkness fell Abe slid painfully from his leafy

perch, pushed his swollen feet into his heavy boots and trudged on. His stomach cramped with hunger and his bruised throat hurt so that he could scarcely swallow. But his burning thirst was hardest to bear. He must find water.

For hours Abe forced one desperate foot after the other. Water—he must have water. The cool night air gave him strength to keep on until a faint gleam of starlight reflected on a shimmering surface, and the hoarse exhortations of a frog to "wa —alk, wa —alk" told him that he neared water.

Gratefully Abe dropped down beside the narrow creek and drank his fill. Ah, that felt better. Now if only he had something to eat. Remembering the hunk of damper left behind in his hut, he shook his head regretfully. No use thinking about that. Or of trying to find anything to eat in the bushland either. He would not find any berries or wild fruits, nothing edible unless he took to eating grubs and lizards like the aborigines did. Abe shuddered. How hungry would a man have to be before he came to that?

With a sigh he straightened up and resumed his half-running, half-walking flight. His injured leg constantly ached.

Birdsong heralded the coming dawn, and Abe again chose a leafy tree well away from the road in which to sleep the daylight hours.

The fourth night of his flight found him almost too weak to walk. Hunger gnawed at his growling stomach. How far had he come? Thirty—forty miles a night? More? Surely he must reach the Donkey Woman's Swamp soon. The shepherd's hut was close to it. He'd be safe there—for a while at least.

Hope and hunger and thirst drove him on through the night. Morning caught him on a barren area that made his heart pound with fear. It had no rock, no tree, no hiding place. Desperately he plodded long the dusty road. No use plunging off to either side.

The sun's glare pained his tired eyes, and he shaded them with his hand, straining into the distance. Was that a hill away ahead? And trees? Yes. His heart leaped. Surely the shepherd's hut was on the other side of that hill and the swamp close by.

Summoning his failing strength he urged his blistered feet forward. The uppers had burst from the soles of his worn boots. His shirt, chest, and arms bore cuts and scratches from many thorny encounters. His unshaven whiskers stuck out like a brush. Anyone seeing him now would take him for a madman or an escaped felon. Perhaps he was both. A bitter cackle escaped him. He hadn't seen or heard a human being on the road since he left Ballarat. If only his luck would hold.

The hill loomed closer—closer. Warily he skirted it. Five hundred yards to the swamp. Two hundred. Abe saw a bird fly down and alight among the reeds. Fifty yards—twenty—ten—

Triumphantly Abe staggered the last few yards and threw himself into the reedy shallows. His cracked lips stung and his swollen tongue scarcely managed to lap the life-saving water.

Wild ducks and swans rustled and honked among the reeds, and in sudden hope Abe felt around the grassy bank in search of a nest. He knew that wild swans nested in August, when winter's cold hand began to release its frosty grip. With luck he might find an egg or two. There were none.

Cursing under his breath, Abe filled his empty stomach with water and half crawled up the hill to the sturdy hut. He saw no sign of the shepherd. Probably the man was miles away with his sheep on another holding. Never mind. Even when he was absent he left a bit of food in his hut.

"Ya never know when some poor cove* might 'appen along and need a bite," he had told the passing drovers. "'S easy enough ter git lost in this 'ere in'ospitable country."

"Well I'm not lost," Abe muttered to himself, "but I'm a poor cove that needs a bite, that's for sure." Cautiously he put his shoulder to the door and stumbled into the hut.

To his starving eyes the small bag of flour and the chunk of salt meat in the shepherd's tucker box looked like bounty. He tore off a bit of meat and chewed it while his shaking hands drew water from the outside rain barrel and mixed some of the flour into dough. A stack of dry wood rested by the fireplace and the shepherd's tinderbox hung from a nail, but it was no

---

* Man, person.

time for baking damper. No, Abe stuffed the sticky mass into his mouth and sighed his gratitude.

When darkness fell Abe checked the shutters over the glassless windows and kindled a small fire. It would keep him warm during the chilly night and he could bake bread in the morning coals. With care the meat and flour would be sufficient for two days, and then——? Abe didn't know.

The fugitive fully extinguished his fire before daylight revealed the telltale smoke, but two nights later he felt, rather than heard, the thudding vibrations of approaching horses.

Troopers! After him! They must be combing the whole countryside. Wildly he leaped off the shepherd's bunk and plunged through the window hole. The shutter banged noisily behind him and he hoped the searchers did not hear it. The horses approached the door of the hut. Madly Abe raced down the back of the hill toward the swamp. If only the men didn't have dogs with them, or a blacktracker, he'd be safe. Darkness and the swamp would hide him.

Panting and stumbling, sweating with fear, Abe reached the marshy fringes and waded into the thick reeds lining the deepest part of the swamp. With nerves stretched to breaking point, he listened for sounds of the troopers. They would know that he had been in the hut—the dying fire would give him away. He hoped they would think that he'd escaped toward Edenhope and try to overtake him in that direction.

The faint sound of a slammed door carried on the still night air; then the thud of hoofbeats grew louder. His heart turned to stone. The men were not leaving, but were returning to water their horses. He sank down among the weeds and reeds until only his head showed.

Eyes and ears straining into the darkness, he heard the horsemen dismount and lead their mounts to the water. For what seemed like hours the horses gulped noisily, and when they finally raised their heads, the men led them away. Abe guessed that they would hobble the horses and let them graze while they boiled the billy and made tea. He groaned inwardly. Maybe they'd unroll their swags and camp close by for the rest of the night.

As if they'd read his thoughts, the two men did exactly that.

To poor Abe Crabtree, trembling among the reeds, no hours had ever seemed so long. He was terrified to move lest he disturb the swans and they give him away, afraid to sleep lest his head slip under water and he drown. To keep awake, he tried to count the myriad stars shining above him.

Not until the first rays of rising sun probed the swamp's clinging mists did the policemen stir, yawn, roll up their swags, and ride off west.

As soon as they had gone out of sight, Abe waded ashore and tried to warm his shivering body and dry his clothes in the strengthening sun. He decided that he had better stay down near the swamp. The police might have left someone to watch the hut. Besides, it was much safer. The surrounding land was as flat as a table. He would see anyone approaching from any direction.

Daylight brought life to the water hole. Birds swooped low in search of insects. Stately swans paddled across its surface, lowering their long, elastic necks to search its muddy depths. Abe knew that the swamp was a favorite nesting place of the great birds, but was it too early in the season? There didn't seem to be many swans around.

Taking a long drink, he tried to ignore his growing hunger. He had water, and that was the main thing. People lived for days, even weeks, without food.

The hot sun beat down on his bare head as he waded around the fringe of the water hole, thrusting the reeds right and left in his search for nests. Twice he found untidy masses of sticks and grass, but no eggs. Weakly he completed his circuit and clasped his hands tightly over his empty stomach. After all, he thought, maybe murderers didn't deserve to eat.

"But I didn't mean to kill him," he protested aloud. "It was in self-defense. That fellow, whoever he was, was choking me."

Still, murder is murder, he reflected. He had no witnesses, and no one would believe his story. They might even think that *he* had stolen the gold he still wore in the belt around his waist.

Murder and theft were not uncommon on the goldfields. It would be no use trying to explain. His only hope was to remain hidden until the police gave up the chase.

Two days later, when he weakly staggered around among the reeds, he found an egg in one of the nests. Tears ran down his cheeks as he clutched the thick-shelled prize to his chest and waded ashore. He cracked the egg on a fallen log and threw his head back to gulp the slimy contents.

Time lost all meaning as one leaden-footed day followed another. Every waking hour flies and biting ants tormented him. At night he huddled close to a fallen log, and mosquitoes pricked him like a thousand red-hot needles. Several times during his weeks of hiding, passing horsemen stopped at the waterhole, and Abe took refuge in the reeds until they departed.

Eventually Abe knew that he could not go on any longer. The occasional egg he found was barely enough to keep him alive. It was twenty—no, twenty-one—days since he'd eaten a proper meal. The weather had changed, too. For the past few days rain had drizzled or poured, and he cowered in cold, wet misery, using the matted reeds as a windbreak against the icy blasts that howled across the exposed swamp area.

His teeth chattered and violent chills racked his skinny frame. It was no use. He would have to give himself up. Hanging would be preferable to such an existence. At least it would be all over and done with quickly. God knew he hadn't meant to kill his attacker.

As soon as darkness fell, Abe headed toward the road. His tattered shirt hung on his emaciated body like rags upon a scarecrow. Myriads of mosquito bites stood out like minute red polka dots on the blue background of his icy skin. His teeth sounded like castanets and he groaned with each agonized, limping step. His wet boots had long ago rotted off his feet.

Abe shuffled over the uneven ground in the direction of the road. Now that he had made up his mind, he didn't care how soon they caught him. How far was it to Edenhope? Fifteen miles? Twenty? He couldn't remember. His brain didn't

function clearly any more. Could he drag himself that far? He
had friends there—Mrs. Molloy at the pub. No, he'd never make
it—he'd die along the way.

Young Mrs. Molloy opened a sleep-heavy eye and peered at
the ornate clock illumined by the faint glow of the night lamp. It
was 2:00 A.M. Was she hearing things? Surely no one was
knocking. Not even the thirstiest drover or happiest miner
would come to the hotel wanting a drink at this hour. Must be
the dogs rattling around. Then, easing her plump body deeper
into the bed, she heard it again. A hesitant tap-tapping and a
faint call:

"Mrs. Molloy! Mrs. Molloy! Please let me in."

"Gracious me! Somebody must be ill." With surprising
agility for her size, the woman sprang out of bed, draped a
faded wrapper over her flannel nightgown, and turned up the
lamp. The wooden stairs creaked under her heavy tread and
she set the lamp carefully on the kitchen table before putting
her hand on the heavy iron door bolt.

"Who is it?" she demanded. She'd better be a bit careful,
what with her Patrick away from home an' all.

"It's me, Abraham Crabtree," a weak voice answered.
"Please let me in."

"What's the matter with ye, man?" She opened the door
and caught the half-collapsing, seminaked man, and helped
him to a canvas chair. "Sure, ye're half frozen, that ye are. And
yer legs is all bleedin'. Did ye crawl here?"

"Part of the way."

Mrs. Molloy dragged a rough gray blanket out of a tin box
and threw it around him. Then she bustled about, stirring up
the fire in the big, black stove and pouring hot water into a tub.
"There, stick yer feet into that and warm 'em." She bustled into
the bar and came out with a small glass of brandy. "An' warm
yer insides up with that while I get ye somethin' to eat. Ye look
starved, that ye do, an' half dead."

Between mouthfuls of fried eggs and bacon Abe told the
kind-hearted Irish woman his story. Beginning with the fearful
awakening with a thief straddling him, right through to where

he could stand his fugitive existence no longer and decided to give himself up.

Mrs. Molloy nodded. "Ye done right, Abe. Ye couldn't stay hidin' in them reeds forever. But there's no hurry. The police can wait awhile longer. Ye'd die if they stuck ye into the clink right now. Hang around here a few days an' get some meat on yer bones. Besides"—she looked him straight in the eye—"if what ye've told me is true, it weren't murder. It were self-defense."

"It *is* true," Abe swore vehemently. "It's all true."

For three days he remained hidden in the cellar of Mrs. Molloy's hotel. She dosed him with rum and milk and fed him like a king. Also she clothed him in one of her husband's shirts and a pair of well-patched breeches. On the fourth morning she told him he'd better go back to Ballarat and give himself up to the police.

"Ole Bill 'Enty's goin' that way with 'is bullock cart. Ye could hitch a ride with 'im—'e is in the bar now."

Abe Crabtree nodded. Now that the time had come, his trembling legs scarcely supported him. He tried to express his gratitude, but Mrs. Molloy would have none of it. " 'Tis naught," she said. "Ye'd do the same for me. I know ye would."

Then Abe took off his canvas belt with the gold dust still intact, and asked her to keep it for him.

"Take out what I owe you for board," he said. "And if I don't ever come back, keep the rest. It's all yours."

"Nonsense!" She picked up the belt. "I'll keep it safe for ye. Off ye go now. Ye can pay me when ye come back." Flapping her apron, she shooed him off as she would a persistent chicken.

Mrs. Molloy's matter-of-fact optimism failed to encourage Abe, and in black despair he crouched on the wooden seat beside old Bill Henty. All during the long miles back to Ballarat dark thoughts chased one another through his anxious mind. What if the policeman did not believe him? Abe really did not have much hope that he would. How could he when he had no witnesses? No, Abe just knew that he'd be thrown into jail, tried, and "hung by the neck until dead." In imagination he heard the judge's sonorous voice pronouncing the sentence, and he shuddered.

"Where d' yer want ter go?" Old Bill inquired the next morning as the cart creaked heavily into the busy mining town. "The pub?"

"No. I have some business at the police station. Thanks for the ride." Abe swung down from the slow-moving vehicle and crossed the road.

Police Constable Bland sat on a wooden chair behind a long table piled high with official-looking papers, his rifle propped conveniently against his knees. He looked up as Abe's figure in the station doorway momentarily blotted out the sunlight.

"I've come to give myself up," Crabtree gulped.

Without showing the least surprise the policeman motioned him to a bench close by the table, and Abe collapsed onto it, shaking.

"Now, what's all this about?" As the policeman absent-mindedly rattled the handcuffs in his pocket, Abe shuddered and gritted his teeth.

"My name's Abraham Crabtree. I'm wanted for murder. About a month ago, here on the diggings, I killed a man who——"

The policeman held up a hand and silenced his confession. A grim smile twitched the corners of his mustache. "We've been wondering where you got to, Abe. Been looking for you all over the place." He stopped and shuffled the pile of papers, picking out one here and there, deliberately delaying his reply. "Actually, we don't want you for murder at all."

The blood drained from Abe's face. "But I——" A lump in his throat prevented further words.

Police Constable Bland tilted his chair back and folded his hands across his chest. "Tom Lester, the fellow you shot—a bad egg, really—didn't die. But he thought he was going to. He bled like a stuck pig, and he was bellowing and calling for a priest when they brought him in here. We fetched a priest out from town, and Tom confessed to him that he had planned to kill you and steal your gold." The policeman eyed Abe sternly. "You were a fool to have that much on you. That's only inviting trouble. Anyway, Tom recovered, so there's no charge against you."

After that experience Abe lost all taste for gold mining. He went back to Mrs. Molloy in Edenhope and turned his gold dust into cash. Then he purchased two fine horses, a saddle, and camping equipment, and set off west to search for work. It wasn't hard to find. Goldrush fever had drained the work force, and the big farm and station owners had a hard time obtaining help. An Irishman named Fallon who owned the big Muller sheep station, hired him.

"Ten bob a week and tucker," Mr. Fallon offered, "and you can doss [sleep] in the shed with the drovers."

But when Mrs. Fallon saw the new station hand she objected. "You'll be wasting your money on that skinny creature," she told her husband. "He looks as if he's never done a decent day's work in his life. Put him on contract jobs."

Abe gladly accepted the change. He toiled early and late, and soon became the highest-paid worker on the Muller station.

Like all the other men on Australian farms and stations, he quickly learned to turn his hand to anything. At shearing time he joined the others in rounding up the flocks and driving them to the shearing sheds. He shepherded the shorn sheep from one pasture to another and helped out in the lambing season. If the sheep did not need attention, he worked in the bush felling trees and splitting the timber for fencing posts.

Whatever Abe did, he did it with all his might. He thought himself lucky to land a congenial job so quickly, particularly when the first day he went up to the station homestead he met Mary Ann.

It was love at first sight. His joy, like a river in flood, knew no bounds when time proved that she reciprocated his feelings. Bright-eyed, red-haired Mary Ann, more than twenty years his junior, loved him, too.

But Abraham quickly realized that the Fallons did not welcome his attentions to their oldest daughter. The courting progressed in secret, and when at last Abe considered the time ripe to approach Fallon and ask for his daughter's hand, he received the anticipated response.

"What?" the irate father roared. "Who do you think you are? You old vagabond, you! Marry my daughter? You—you—you *boundary rider!* Where would you keep her? In your saddlebag, eh? No, Mary Ann's used to things a lot better than you could give her.* Besides"—and it was his parting shot—"we're all good Catholics here, and we won't have our daughter marrying any—any Protestant heretic!" He spat the final words.

"Very well, sir. I'll leave tomorrow." Inclining his head respectfully, Abe stalked out of the room. Mary Ann, listening at the keyhole of the opposite door, burst into tears and fled.

"That's what father always does," she sobbed to her sympathetic younger sister. "He frightens off all our suitors. None of us will get married—ever."

But love finds a way. Not many weeks later, on a dark, moonless night, Abe rode up to the boundary gates of Muller station. Silent as a shadow he dismounted and tied his two thoroughbred horses—one of them equipped with a brand-new sidesaddle—to the fence. Then he crept quietly up to the house and whistled softly outside the French doors that led from the wide veranda into Mary Ann's bedroom. In a moment she appeared with a few of her personal belongings tied up in a bundle, and the two ran swiftly down to the waiting horses.

By the time her furious father located the runaways it was too late. The Reverend Collins of the local Anglican church had declared them man and wife.

Abraham and Mary Ann Crabtree set up housekeeping in a primitive farmhouse at Lemon Springs, twenty miles north of Booroopki.

Apart from his loyalty and love, Abe had little else to offer his bride. He had no money in the bank, owned no farm, and possessed no animals other than his thoroughbred horses.

---

* In later years the Fallons fell on hard times. Mr. Fallon died, and Mrs. Fallon and an unmarried daughter were glad enough to end their days as permanent guests in Abe and Mary Ann's humble home.

But despite his lame leg he could walk as fast as any man and work as hard as two. She would never know want while he was alive.

At intervals during the first years of their married life, Abe went back to droving. It offered good money, though it was hard work and meant leaving Mary Ann and the children alone for weeks—sometimes months—on end. Not that she had any difficulty in coping. Her country upbringing qualified her to deal with any emergency, from an outbreak of measles to killing the snake that insisted on curling up in the rafters of their barn.

Whenever Abe went off on a droving trip, Mary Ann accompanied him to the road. Droving was not especially dangerous work, not as prone to accident as logging or mustering, but one never knew—particularly after what had happened to his leg on a former trip.

Abe waved his whip in goodbye and she waved back and sighed. When horse and man disappeared in a cloud of dust, she crossed herself and turned back to the house.

"Well, that's the way it goes," she muttered, swishing at the flies with a twig of gum leaves. "Men must work and women must worry." She crossed herself again, and when she entered their two-room shack, she knelt by the bed and said a "Hail Mary" before beginning her tasks.

At other times Abe took seasonal work with Squire Broughton, their nearest neighbor. But they were not happy experiences. The two Englishmen clashed on every possible occasion.

The squire, a wealthy, God-fearing wool grower with impeccable manners and integrity, respected Abe as a hard worker, but resented his fierce pride, fiery temper, and, above all, his Jack's-as-good-as-his-master attitude. On his part Abe despised Mr. Broughton's affluence and influence in the district and liked nothing better than to "take his nibs down a peg or two."

Probably a psychologist would have diagnosed Abe's animosity as deep-seated jealousy, but Freud lived on the other side of the world from Booroopki and was still only a child when Crabtree and Broughton maintained their feud.

Abe's oldest son, David, was born with turned-in feet. Back in 1868 the district had no doctor, and the neighbor woman who acted as midwife said, "Tut tut, poor little mannie has bumble feet." But she could do nothing about it.

As he grew, the little fellow learned to creep and then to walk, shuffling unsteadily along, falling more often than he was upright. Finally, it became evident that the situation would not improve, so Abe did something about it.

With the help of the local blacksmith, he fashioned a pair of iron boots for his little son. Whether he delved back into his youth in England and remembered seeing lame children wearing similar things or originated the idea himself, no one knows.

For years the child endured the taunts and tortures those boots occasioned. Then, one day when he was about 8 years old, Mr. Broughton's gardener met him hobbling along the road, trying to round up a straying cow.

"Come over here, son," the man called.

People stood slightly in awe of Mr. Fairburn. He was new to the district, but his precise English speech and gentleman's hands hinted of a past. Australia knew many such men. Respected, even titled, families had those who, because of some grievous misdemeanor or their fondness for the bottle, were hustled out to the colony. Some of them received a small monthly remittance from the family fortunes on condition that they remain away from England, lest they bring further disgrace to their illustrious relatives.

Probably, the locals speculated, Mr. Fairburn was one of these. Certainly no one could deny his fondness for liquor. Even when sober he was practically useless as a worker.

Mr. Broughton was well aware of the mystery surrounding Fairburn, but he generously allowed him a room and tucker in return for his somewhat unreliable services as a gardener.

"Take your boots off. I want to have a look at your feet."

Nervously David obeyed. One didn't question an adult's

orders. Besides, Mr. Fairburn's voice was kind and he certainly was not drunk at the moment.

The gardener dropped on his knees in the dust and took David's right foot in his hand. Gently he turned it from side to side, manipulating the ankle with strong, slender fingers. He put the right foot down and reached for the left, turning it this way and that, frowning slightly in deep concentration. Then he looked into David's eyes, smiled, and said, "Put your boots on and come up to the house with me."

The boy's anxious gaze flew to the cow. She grazed quietly enough now, but would she wander away again during his absence? "I'll tie her up." While David struggled to fasten his iron boots Fairburn secured the cow to a nearby tree. Then man and boy walked the short distance to Mr. Broughton's house.

He saw them coming and stepped down from the veranda. "Anything wrong, Fairburn? Has this boy been into mischief?"

Ignoring the questions, his employee came right to the point. "If I had the proper instruments I could straighten his feet."

"You?" Shock relaxed the man's jaw, and the pipe fell from his mouth. When he bent to retrieve it, tobacco ash spilled over his fingers. Impatiently he flicked his hand. "What do you know about surgery, Fairburn?"

In answer, the gardener stalked off to the shed where he had his room. Mr. Broughton stared after him, sucking absently on his empty pipe. David hung his head, eyes fastened shyly on the toes of his hated boots. He wished with all his heart that he was safe at home. What did Mr. Fairburn mean anyway? How could anyone straighten his crooked feet?

In a few minutes Fairburn returned. Without saying a word he handed Broughton a framed certificate.

His employer's bushy eyebrows shot up. " 'Royal College of Surgeons, London,' " he muttered. He read and reread the certificate. Then he stared at his gardener. "So you're a doctor, eh, Fairburn? A surgeon."

"Yes."

"Drink brought you out here, eh?"

"Yes."

A look of pity softened his steely eyes as he glanced over the edge of the certificate at Mr. Fairburn.

"A great pity. Well——"

They spent some time talking back and forth, something about cutting tendons and releasing tensions. David did not understand any of it. Finally, Broughton said, "We'll have to speak to his father. It will take time to get the instruments out from England, but if you'll give me the details, I'll take care of that."

The green leaves on the district's solitary row of poplars turned gold, then red, brown, and finally the branches stood stark and bare, before the instruments arrived.

But one day the arrangements were all completed, and a nervous boy and an equally apprehensive Mary Ann accompanied Abe to the wealthy man's house. Fairburn would perform the operation on the large wooden table in Squire Broughton's spacious kitchen, and the shining instruments already lay in terrifying array on a small side table. Mr. and Mrs. Broughton and others crowded around the doors. David's fears mounted.

"Come along, sonny." Fairburn held out his hand.

With a last despairing look into his mother's anxious eyes, David clambered onto the table.

The operation proved successful beyond the family's wildest hopes. After lying in bed for weeks, his bandaged feet regularly examined by Dr. Fairburn, David stood up and took a few faltering steps. He walked slowly at first, under the careful tutelage of the erstwhile gardener, then faster. Joyously the boy threw away his iron boots and skipped barefoot.

To the end of his long life David had flat feet. But that was no reflection on Fairburn's skill. An inherited disability, it showed up here and there in generations of Crabbtyres.

The district soon buzzed with the story of Dr. Fairburn's skill. Although he never put out his shingle and was always known as Squire Broughton's gardener, Dr. Fairburn became a household word in that isolated farming community. He was a clever, upright, kindly man when not drunk, and the tales of his cures became legion.

On one occasion Bill, a disillusioned gold miner turned farmhand, stacked hay on a farm several miles from Lemon Springs. Somehow he slipped off the top of the high stack and slithered down it to land with all his force on a hayfork sticking upright into the ground below.

Fortunately for Bill, the fork tines were well embedded in the earth, but the speed of his fall and his body weight broke the fork handle and the jagged end of wood pierced his body.

The horrified farmer and the other workers quickly decided that it was no case for bush doctoring. They dispatched a messenger on the fastest horse available. "Go to Mr. Broughton's house and tell his gardener to come quick. Tell him what's happened to Bill."

In the shortest possible time Fairburn galloped up on one of Mr. Broughton's thoroughbreds and took charge of the situation. "Get me some charcoal and crush it into powder," he directed the farmer's wife. "And a sheet for bandaging."

While willing hands held the groaning, injured man still, Dr. Fairburn gently removed the fork handle and poured the powdered charcoal into the ugly wound.

"Stay in bed for a couple of weeks, mate," he instructed the ashen-faced farmhand. "You'll be as good as new when that hole heals." He drew the sheet bandage tightly around his patient's middle.

The other men quickly fashioned a bush stretcher out of their coats and a couple of saplings and carried Bill up to his bunk. The charcoal did its work well. Inside a month Bill returned to work with a scar to show and a tale to tell.

THE END OF HOPPING
ABE

Five children arrived to bless the Crabtree household. First came David, then Frank, Carolyn, and finally Jack and Henry.

When Henry was not much more than an infant the traveling priest called at their home. His vast circuit kept his visits years apart.

Abe cared little for religion. He had long ago promised Mary Ann that she could bring up the children as Roman Catholics, for all he minded. So when Father O'Shannessy rode up to the house to give them his blessing, she seized the opportunity to have all the children baptized.

He sprinkled Frank, Carrie, Jack, and Henry from his seemingly inexhaustible flask of holy water; then Mrs. Crabtree pushed David forward.

"What age is this boy?" Father O'Shannessy asked.

"Seven years," Mary Ann responded. A proud smile lighted her tired eyes as she gazed at her firstborn.

"Does he know his catechism?"

She gasped. "Know his catechism? Of course not, Father. There is no——"

"Then I cannot baptize him until he does. He is not a baby. He is old enough to——"

"Then he can be a Protestant like his father," Mary Ann broke in with a flash of her former independent spirit.

And a Protestant David Crabtree remained until the end of his long life.

About two years later Abe decided that it was time he put down roots and established something permanent for his wife and growing children. He had been working for more than a decade in the Goroke district, and he did not own an acre.

"There's lots of good land around Charligrark Lake, Mary Ann. I think I'll take up a selection around there. Yes, I know Mr. Broughton runs his sheep and cattle on it, but that doesn't mean that it is *his*. Anyone can peg out a claim and take up a selection."

"You'd better be sure," Mary Ann cautioned. "He's been very kind to David. I'd hate to upset him and——"

"Kind or not, he has no right to the land any more than I have. He's been running his sheep on it for years. It's about time someone else got a look in."

Next morning Abe saddled his horse and rode in to Edenhope to ask the man at the Lands Department about the particular area he had in mind. As he thought, the area was still Crown land. No one had staked it out or claimed it.

"Then there's nothing to prevent me from taking up a holding there?"

"No. Not so long as you comply with the usual requirements." The Lands official stroked his chin and stared contemplatively at him before he added, "No, nothing at all—except Mr. Broughton."

Huh, I'll take care of him, Abe thought, but he said nothing. Instead he hurried home to tell his wife the news. That same evening he set to work, axing the necessary wooden pegs into shape, and the next day he rode around and marked out approximately two hundred acres for a farm.

It did not take long for someone to carry the news to Mr. Broughton. He owned a stud sheep farm, and the biggest house and garden in the district. Besides that, he ran his stock on thousands of acres of unfenced farmland that belonged to no one, supposedly free for the taking. But Mr. Broughton saw to it that no one other than himself ever got a foothold. Jumping onto his horse, he rode along Abe's boundary and personally pulled out every peg that Abe had hammered in and burned them.

Abe had expected it. The next day, with the glint of battle in his eye, he loaded his old dray up with axes, ropes, and saw, hitched the working mare into the shafts, and with 10-year old David to assist, he drove back to the area.

It took a whole day of hard work, but between them they managed to lop the branches off enough sturdy saplings to form natural boundary pegs.

"Now, let's see him pull those out!" The older Crabtree chuckled grimly.

He felt pleased with himself. In fact, so pleased that he sent a verbal challenge to Mr. Broughton. The neighbor who carried it knocked on the squire's door and blurted out to the landowner, "Abe says he'd like to see you pull those pegs out and burn them."

A confrontation was inevitable. Dueling was still the gentlemanly way of settling an argument, and Abe met Broughton with a loaded revolver at his hip and a dagger in his hand. "Choose your weapon," he invited proudly, feeling that he was a nineteenth-century personification of his family coat of arms.

"You—you—so and so!" Mr. Broughton roundly cursed all selectors* in general and Abraham Crabtree in particular. He wanted no duel. All he wanted was to have every small farmer wiped off the face of Australia. Becoming more furious by the minute, he raved on and on.

"Aw, shut yer trap and go to hell!" Abe said. Sheathing his dagger, he wheeled his horse and galloped off.

Mr. Broughton looked as if he were about to burst. Instead, he turned his horse around and whipped the startled animal off in the direction of Edenhope. The last the fascinated onlookers saw of him was the rhythmic rising and falling of his whip hand until a cloud of dust swallowed him up.

Two days later the local policeman and his offsider† appeared on Abe's doorstep. "Look here, Crabtree," the policeman began, "we don't want to arrest you. We know you've got a wife and five children to support. But you can't go around telling a gentleman like Mr. Broughton to go to hell. It's an offense against the law, and Mr. Broughton has laid a charge against you."

---

* Under the Australian land laws one who selected land—a small farmer.
† Helper or assistant.

The policeman cleared his throat. "Now, what I suggest"—he glanced uneasily at Abe, as though expecting stiff resistance—"what I suggest is that we ride over to Mr. Broughton's house and you tell him that you're sorry that you said that. I'm sure that he will accept your apology, we can drop the charges, and that will be the end of the matter."

The law official stared fixedly at a spot on the wall behind Abe's head while he waited for an answer. His offsider nervously studied the toes of his boots. He seemed to find something intensely interesting in the pattern of dust across the heavy leather. Both men knew of Abe's unpredictable temper.

"Oh, well." Abe ran his hand through his shock of unkempt hair. "Oh, well, I suppose I could do that for you."

"Right." The policeman sighed his relief. "Let's go there straight away and get it over with."

Abe mounted his horse, and the three of them clopped along the dirt track that led to the station homestead. At the front gate they alighted and Crabtree tied the horses to the hitching post while the policemen went to the door.

Broughton appeared in answer to their knock and the constable touched his cap respectfully. "We've brought Mr. Crabtree up to talk to you, sir. We hope a settlement can be arranged between you two—er—gentlemen."

"Bring the fellow* in." The squire looked disdainfully down his nose. "Bring him in."

At a signal from the policeman Abe hop-bounded up the steps and followed the three men into the house. Mr. Broughton motioned them to seats in the small room known as his office. An unnatural silence settled over the group, and the squire tapped impatiently on the arm of his chair. The two policemen glanced at each other and then at Abe.

Coughing loudly, Abe turned to face Broughton. "I understand you have laid a charge against me. What is it about?"

The other man's face reddened, and it seemed to be an effort for him to remain seated. His fists clenched and

---

* A disparaging word implying that the man was a sheep stealer.

unclenched. "You know very well that you told me to go to hell."

Calmly Abe stared at him. "Oh, yes. So I did. I recall that now." His cool gaze never left Broughton's face. "Well, that was three days ago, and seeing that you haven't gone there yet, I say now that you need not go at all."

With that he nodded courteously to the two policemen, limped out to his horse, and rode back home. As far as he was concerned the matter was closed. But it was by no means the end. As the years went by the wealthy squatter* lost no opportunity to make things difficult for him, or any other farmer who took up selections on "his" land.

Despite this, Abe went ahead and constructed a sturdy brick house on his selection. With his sons' help he molded local clay into bricks, which he burned to a hardness that survived for nearly a hundred years.

The bricks prevented what could have been a terrible tragedy.

One particular afternoon, long after the family had moved into the new house, Mr. Broughton and his groom rode across to Charligrark Lake to shoot swans. They were on the opposite side of the lake and about half a mile from the Crabtree homestead, and all might have gone well if every bullet had brought down a swan. Inevitably, some of their shots missed. The bullets ricocheted off the water and zipped straight into the walls of Abe's house. It happened so often that Mary closed the shutters, and she and the children cowered inside, too terrified to move outdoors lest a stray bullet cut them down.

When Abe came in from his plowing and found out what was wrong he stamped out to the shed and took his old muzzleloader down from the wall. With mounting fury he oiled the barrel and rammed in a charge. Then he braved the whining bullets and chose a vantage point from where he could see the hunters.

Bang! Abe was a crack shot. The charge from his gun whistled past Mr. Broughton's ear.

"Where did that come from?" The squire jumped and

---

* The owner or occupant of a large sheep ranch, or station, in Australia.

turned pale.

Bang! The second shot hit a tree behind him.

Now Mr. Broughton knew. "It's that so-and-so selector shooting at us!" he fumed. "That mad, sandy-headed Englishman!" With the groom at his heels, he stormed across the paddocks at the end of the lake and charged toward Abe's house.

"What do you mean by shooting at us?" he demanded. "Don't you know that I could have the law on you?"

"And what do you mean by shooting in my direction? Don't you know that you could have killed my wife or one of my children? Just take a look, sir, at all your bullet holes in the walls of my house."

Crabtree led the unwilling men around and pointed out the bullets lodged in various parts of his house. "There's one. And there's another. And another in here close to the window." Abe pointed to the depression in the brick. "If it had gone right through——" He left the sentence unfinished.

Mr. Broughton's face reddened and his lips thinned into lines of angry frustration. Without a word he and his groom turned and strode back to the lake.

For some obscure reason the episode ended their feud. With the passing years the two men observed a truce that gradually developed into tolerance.

By the time old age overtook them and they sold their respective holdings to younger men, the two former enemies had become amicable neighbors.

After the children grew up and left home Abe settled into something less strenuous than farmwork. He and Mary Ann moved to Booroopki* settlement, not far from Edenhope and only twenty miles from the South Australian border. Here Abe became the proprietor of the Border Inn, or Halfway House, as people more commonly called it, where Cobb & Co. coaches changed horses on the long journey between Melbourne and Adelaide.

As early as 1851 James Watt and James Crook had begun regular coach services between Melbourne and the Ballarat

* An Aboriginal word meaning "the land of big trees," in this case, red gums.

goldfields. But it was Freeman Cobb, an enterprising American, who crisscrossed eastern Australia with his coaching services. For seventy years, until finally ousted by the motorcar, Cobb & Co. coach services maintained· a high degree of efficiency. They kept to a rigid timetable with their transport of passengers, goods, and mail. In fact, the post office imposed heavy fines on the drivers if the mails were more than ten minutes late in arriving.

In order to uphold their reputation, Cobb & Co. established changing stations every ten to thirty miles, depending on the type of country the horses traveled. Rough, hilly routes required fresh teams of horses more frequently than did smooth, flat plains.

Some of the stations were little more than a shed for housing the groom and harness, and a paddock for grazing the horses. Others, such as the Border Inn, were regular stopping places, where passengers alighted to eat and drink and refresh themselves—even stay overnight if the timetable dictated it. The drivers exchanged mailbags, and the inn proprietor served as the local postmaster, as well.

At every station, as the time appointed for the coach's arrival approached, the groom mustered his team of horses and had them collared and blinkered, all ready to take over the coach as soon as the men had the tired horses unharnessed. Most change paddocks ran a team of five to seven horses, plus a few in reserve in case of illness or accident.

One bright morning when Abe limped out to tend his coach horses he found a strange colt running alongside the fence. The young animal raced back and forth, whinnying, eyeing the horses inside the yard, seemingly eager to join them. At Abe's approach the colt tossed his head and galloped off.

But when Abe opened the gate and moved in among the horses, the colt trotted confidently into the paddock and helped himself to food and water along with the rest.

"I can't find out who he belongs to," Abe told his wife a few days later. "I've asked everyone around, but no one has heard of a missing black colt.

"Well, I suppose he'd better stay here until someone claims him."

"I suppose so."

When several weeks passed and still no one showed up to announce himself as the animal's owner, Abe began breaking in the colt for riding and pulling a cart.

Unfortunately, Abe did not leave all his enemies behind when he left the farm. He was the type of person who could not be ignored or merely tolerated. People either hated him or they were his friends.

So, when they noticed the black colt continuing to run in Crabtree's paddock, some of the locals who held grudges against him saw a chance to get even. They sent false reports to those in authority, and, acting on their information, two detectives came up from Melbourne. Posing as buyers, they visited several farmers in the district, ostensibly on the lookout for good riding horses, and that night they put up at the Border Inn hostelry.

Next morning the two men wandered out to the paddock and watched Abe at work with the coach horses. "Nice bunch of animals you have there," the first horse buyer remarked.

"Yes," Abe agreed. "I like a good horse. But most of these belong to the company."

"M'mm." The second man lounged against the fence rails and chewed on a grass stalk. "That black colt is too young for a coach horse. He's a real beauty. Would you consider selling him, Mr. Crabtree?"

Abe thought for a while. "Ye—es. I suppose I could sell him."

"Right." The two men clambered over the rails, and Abe cornered the flighty animal and held him for their inspection. They ran their hands over the colt's shiny flanks and pried his mouth open to examine his teeth. After a little dickering they agreed upon a price.

"We've got to go on to Edenhope now, but we'll be back with the money tomorrow," they promised, "and we'll take delivery of the colt then."

Instead, the next day the two "horse buyers" returned to the Border Inn with a warrant for Abe's arrest as a horse thief. Despite his protests and explanations, they marched him off to Edenhope. Mary Ann went along, too, weeping copiously. Of all the troubles that she had endured, this was the ultimate. The shame of it—her husband accused of being a horse thief!

The authorities allowed Abe bail, and he and his wife returned home the same day. A few months later when the Horsham court opened for the trial, Abe brought a barrister up from Melbourne to plead his case.

Abe's defense was that he had not *offered* the black colt for sale. He had only acceded to the detective's request. True, he had set a price, but he considered it merely as reimbursement for the food and care that he had given the black colt. Besides, who *did* own the animal? No one had ever come forward to claim him. And no one showed up now, either. The judge dismissed the case.

He had his name cleared, but his enemies waited for their next chance.

Some time later—whether months or years, no one recollects now—the local policeman came to the inn with another warrant for his arrest. "I've got you now, Abe," he gloated as he locked handcuffs on Crabtree's unresisting wrists. "In the past you've always had the best of me, but this time I'm going to put you in jail. Come on, mount that old mare of yours and get going."

"You haven't got me yet." Abe set his jaw.

"Oh, yes, I have. Kick your old mare into line alongside mine. I'll lead her with this rope. You won't get away this time."

"I won't get away, eh?"

"No. Not this time. Come along. Keep her up with my horse."

Obediently Abe dug his heels into the mare's fat belly, and she put on an obliging burst of speed, but soon she lagged behind again.

"Come on." The trooper tugged the lead rope impatiently.

"Hurry up."

Once more Crabtree kicked the mare, and she amiably jogged a few yards before falling back into her usual lazy pace.

Not far from Edenhope the track wound through tangled masses of thick ti-tree scrub. Abe waited until they rode through the middle of it and the mare was ambling along with the full length of the lead rope between her and the policeman. Then he quietly slipped his feet out of the stirrups and with a quick sideways move, lurched off the horse and scuttled into the trees. The policeman heard the snapping twigs and whirled around in his saddle.

"Stop! You so-and-so fool! Stop or I'll shoot you!"

But by the time he reined in both horses and reached for his gun, Abe had vanished. The officer fired into the bushes, but it was useless, and the furious man could do nothing but continue into Edenhope, leading Abe's mare with her empty saddle as mute evidence of his prisoner's escape.

Abe was as fully at home in the bush as a kangaroo and knew the fuming policeman had no hope of finding him. Chuckling to himself, he took his direction from the sun and pushed his way through the dense scrub. Hour after hour he limped back toward the Border Inn.

Late in the afternoon Abe heard the distant thud of ax blows. He frowned. Probably it was a woodcutter splitting bark for roofing shingles, but he'd better make sure the man was alone.

Silently he approached the sound and peered between the trees. Yes, he spotted only one man working in a small clearing. Abe broke over and limped across the log-littered ground.

"Good afternoon," he greeted the startled woodcutter. The man nodded a surprised acknowledgment as Abe walked toward him and laid his manacled hands on the nearest stump. "Here, chop this chain apart, will you?"

The woodcutter goggled at him. What escaped felon was this?

"I daren't," he trembled. "Those handcuffs are the queen's

property."

"Chop it!" Crabtree roared.

The terrified man brought his ax down, severing the chain with one mighty blow.

"Thanks."

Now that he could move his hands freely, Abe reached down and took one of the leather laces out of his boots. He threaded it through the handcuffs and with a bit of clever maneuvering succeeded in slipping them off his wrists.

Thrusting the manacles into his pocket, Abe bade the gaping woodcutter goodbye and set off. Since it was too late to reach home before dark, he headed for his friend Nixon's house.

Nixon showed no surprise when Crabtree trudged out of the darkness. He and Abe had known each other a long time. The man lived on the borderline of respectability. Nobody ever proved anything against him, but local gossip had it that Nixon was the man who passed on news of police movements to Gardiner,* the notorious bushranger. "He's the gang's thirteenth man," the whisperers said. "Probably they pay him with a share of the spoil when they rob a coach. Who knows?"

If Abe did, he kept his mouth shut. Now Nixon greeted him with a hearty slap on the back and laughed uproariously when Abe told his story and produced the severed handcuffs.

"We'll show that bright boy a thing or two. Come on out to the workshop."

Working together, the pair forged a new link and mended the severed handcuffs. "That link looks too bright and new." Nixon frowned at the shiny link. "I know." He fetched the teapot off the back of the kitchen stove. "If we steep those handcuffs in cold tea overnight, no one will know the difference."

Next morning Abe and his friend rode into Edenhope, where Crabtree returned the handcuffs to the chagrined policeman. "I suppose, while I'm here, I'd better give myself up too," he said. "What's the charge you've got against me this time?"

"No charge," the officer muttered. "It was all a mistake."

---

* Gardiner was a well-known leader of a gang of twelve outlaws.

Abe's eyebrows shot up. He opened his mouth to say something and then shut it again. Perhaps he'd better not further humiliate the law.

But Nixon had no such qualms, badgering the officer until he found out that one of Abe's enemies had laid a trumped-up charge in order to disgrace and shame the untamable Hopping Abe.

But once again Abe had the last laugh. He refused to tell how he had managed to slip the still-locked handcuffs off his wrists. Not until after his death did the story leak out.

On the days that they expected the mail coach, lads from the outlying farms and stations congregated at the Border Inn to collect their mail and whatever news they could garner from the coachman and passengers. But once the coach departed and he had distributed the mail, Abe did not like them hanging around. They raced their horses and cracked their whips. That and the shouting and high-spirted showing off could too easily lead to accidents or fights.

"Get off home with you!" he bellowed at them. "You've got your mail. Now get going or I'll pepper you with lead." If they did not leave quickly enough, he grabbed his old shotgun and sent a shower of pellets through the porthole in his door.

The way Abe discharged his duties satisfied most people, but a few, including Sam Lancaster, contended that he was not a suitable postmaster. The fact was that Sam wanted the job himself, and he resorted to subterfuge to get it.

One afternoon Lancaster came into the office with a letter that he wanted sent by registered post.

"Right you are, Sam." Laboriously Abe scrawled the address and other particulars in his record book. He rummaged through a drawer full of stamps and government papers until he found a half stick of red sealing wax followed by more searching for a flint box to ignite the tiny burner on his scarred desk. Then he triumphantly held the end of the sealing wax in the flame until two big red blobs of melted wax dropped onto the envelope's flap. With a satisfied grunt Abe pressed a metal seal onto the soft wax and squinted at the imprint.

A few quick strokes with his thick pencil completed the operation. Abe tossed the envelope into a gaping mailbag. "There y' are, Sam. That'll cost you . . ." Crabtree dispatched his post office duties with the same vigor as he tackled everything else.

But that innocent transaction had repercussions.

A few weeks later Sam Lancaster stormed into the post office and accused Abe of being a thief. "That letter you registered was opened!" he shouted. "There was money in it to pay an account. But when it arrived the seals had been tampered with and the money was gone. You're a durned thief, Abe."

Abe was not the kind of man to take such accusations silently. He shouted back, and pretty soon Abe ended up in court again. However, witnesses proved without a shadow of doubt that Lancaster had not put the money in the envelope at all, and Sam lost the case.

The incident did not endear Abe and Sam to each other, and neither of them ever missed an opportunity to attack the other.

The post office, which was really the living room of Abe's house, had to be accessible to all. Therefore Abe had cut a round porthole in the front door so that he could distribute mail and transact other business without having people wandering all through his house. Above the hole there was a large nail to which he fastened the cover when he had it open.

One afternoon, a few months after the court case, Abe sat in his living room sipping rum with some of his cronies when Sam Lancaster appeared at the porthole.

"See here, Abe," he called loudly. "I have a letter to register, and the money is in it too. Look, all of you fellows; you be witnesses."

"Give it here." Abe stomped over to the porthole and grabbed the letter. But Sam hung onto it and his arm came in through the porthole. Thoroughly enraged, Abe dragged him close to the door. Thrusting his fist through the porthole Abe gave Sam a powerful wallop in the eye.

At the same instant he caught his own nose on the projecting nail and tore a deep gash across his nose and up to his forehead. As blood streamed from the wound, Abe seized the opportunity. "See what Sam's done to me!" he shouted to his friends. "Look what this man's done to Her Majesty's servant! He's assaulted me!"

Inevitably the incident led to another court case. The judge convicted Abe and bound him over on the promise of good behavior for three years.

With the passing of time a lot of the fire died out of the old man, especially after Mary Ann's death. He was never the same after that. In fact, the priest who conducted his wife's funeral persuaded him to become a Roman Catholic.

"You can't be buried beside your wife unless you do," he warned. "This is goodbye forever. There is no heaven for you unless you adopt the Roman Catholic religion."

So old Abe let the priest sprinkle him with holy water, and he hung a rosary above his bed and subscribed, outwardly at least, to the tenets of the Roman Catholic Church.

Toward the end of his long life Abe developed cancer in his jaw. Judging by the results, the outback doctor who operated on him was only several degrees removed from a butcher. He hacked a lot of his jaw away and most of his gullet. Abe could scarcely swallow and spent the last few months of his life in agony.

His grandson Tom used to feel sorry for the old man with the drooping mustache that only half hid the terrible scars on his face and neck. Tom's mother, David's wife, showed more kindness to Abe than did the rest of his family. She sat for hours and sewed while she listened to his tales of long ago. As he recounted his youthful exploits she smiled with him, and nodded in sympathy as he recalled the times he'd suffered. Sometimes they laughed and cried together.

Only once does Tom remember his grandfather losing his temper and shouting at his mother like he did at everyone else, and that had to do with the hawker.

Traveling Indian or Afghan salesmen had regular routes in

the outback, and the people anticipated their arrival as eagerly as a trip to town. They rattled up to the gate in covered wagons crammed to the roof with bolts of cloth and boxes of buttons, boots and tools, toys and tinware, and clattering rows of shiny pots and pans dangling on the back.

Abe and the hawker were great friends. After the Indian completed his sales, tucked the money into his wide cloth belt, and rewarded the wide-eyed children with peppermints, Crabtree beckoned mysteriously and the two went off to "wet their whistles."

That particular day was unseasonably hot and the whistles must have needed a lot of wetting. By the time the hawker was ready to leave, Abe had persuaded him that they should exchange headgear. So the Indian staggered off to his cart with Abe's battered cork-trimmed felt hat jammed over his swarthy ears, and Abe limped up to the kitchen with the Indian's yellow turban wound tightly around his gray head. He swayed slightly in the doorway.

"Demmie," he announced solemnly, "I've—I've become a Hindu. What—hic—what do you think of that?"

Tom's mother looked up from the dough she kneaded. "Oh, Grandpa," she laughed, "you look ridiculous. Take that silly hat off."

"Ridiculous?" The old man's temper flared in an instant. "Ridiculous? You call this a silly hat? I'll beat you for that."

The children screamed as he lunged toward his daughter-in-law, and his sons David and Frank rushed in from the yard and overpowered him.

Until illness finally confined him to bed, Abe drove his daughter-in-law to church on Sundays, seven miles there and seven miles back, in an open horse-drawn buggy.

"Why didn't you ever take your wife to church when she was alive?" she asked one day.

The old man sucked on his pipe and flicked the horse with a nonchalant whip. "She never asked me to," he replied with the English accent that he had not lost despite more than half a century in Australia. "I would have taken her if she'd asked me."

Doubtless Tom's mother had her own ideas about the truth of that statement, but she wisely kept them to herself.

In 1906 old Abraham Crabbtyre turned Crabtree died, as wild and untamable as he had lived. But for many years the stories of his exploits survived. Old inhabitants of Booroopki, adding or subtracting as it suited their purpose, told them to their sons and grandsons. With their passing an era died.

Now sheep and cattle in huge, motorized road trains speed along black asphalt ribbons where once Abe and his friends rode horseback as they drove their flocks and herds over rough, dirt trails. Now he and his contemporaries are remembered only in legend.

DAVID AND DAMARIS'
CHILDREN

Whatever Mr. Broughton's opinion of Abe Crabtree might have been, he certainly followed the Biblical injunction that "the son shall not bear the iniquity of the father." * He harbored no grudges against Abe's son David.

In fact, probably because of the part he had played in straightening the child's twisted feet, Broughton took a special interest in him. As soon as the boy was old enough, the squire had him apprenticed to a wool classer.

Wool was, and still is, Australia's principal industry, and anything to do with wool practically assured a man's future. So young David Crabtree learned to judge the qualities of wool fibers.

An experienced wool classer taught him to recognize fiber length and density, to test for elasticity, strength, and luster, and to estimate the weight and value of the fleece obtainable from a sheep.

David took his work seriously, and by the time he was qualified to go on his own, he had built up a reputation for honesty and industry. In a short time his wool-classing services were in great demand on the big sheep stations when thousands of animals were brought in for the annual spring shearing.

The men did most of the shearing with hand clippers, and an expert could handle more than a hundred sheep in a day. An air of excitement pervaded the dusty shearing sheds, where sweating men bent over the thick-fleeced sheep, their clicking shears working with lightning speed as each tried to outdo the other. Jackaroos† scurried back and forth, herding an endless

*Ezekiel 18:20.
†An apprentice rancher.

supply of the woolly creatures into holding pens and, afterward, driving the skinny caricatures out another door.

"Tar!"

That urgent summons from any one of the shearers brought the tar boy running with his brush and bucket, ready with a healing dab for the spot where the hurrying shears had bitten into a sheep's flesh.

The shearers worked from early morning until it was too dark to see what they were doing. Then they tallied up their scores, and there was not a little quiet pride when someone equaled or surpassed another's record.

Although, by virtue of his profession, David Crabtree had more prestige than the shearers and ordinary farmhands, he enjoyed working in the busy atmosphere of the sheds and had no desire to be anything but an itinerant wool classer—until he met Damaris Marsh.

The Marsh family came out from England in the middle of the nineteenth century. Mr. Marsh and his older sons found work with the famous Henty brothers, farmers who owned so much land between Portland and Hamilton in Victoria that it took sixteen weeks for a pair of bullocks yoked to a plow to mark the boundaries of their holding.

Damaris, one of the three Marsh girls, was 15 years old when in 1885, her cousin, who had newly come to Australia, converted her to the Salvation Army religion. "You won't be able to wear a uniform and play a tambourine, because there are so few Salvationists out here," her cousin John said seriously. "But you can be a true soldier of Christ in the midst of a wicked and perverse generation."

Blue-eyed Demmie accepted the challenge. For seventy-two years she upheld the Army banner, and did her best to influence others for Christ.

Perhaps it was her quiet dedication, reminding him of his Catholic mother, that attracted David Crabtree to Damaris. Certainly it was not that he shared her love for spiritual things. He had inherited more than his share of his father's fiery nature, though Mary Ann's gentleness tempered it somewhat, and he kept it under control outside of the home. All of Abe's sons and daughters managed to stay out of trouble and gradually live down the notorious reputation of old Hopping Abe, but none of them impressed anyone by their piety.

Damaris liked David, too, and their courtship progressed with suitable Victorian chaperonage and propriety.

At 25, David had a regular seasonal income and a little "put by." His prospects were better than most of the drovers and struggling young farmers in the district. Mr. Marsh didn't hesitate when the young man formally asked for his daughter's hand in marriage. "Of course, David, my boy. I know Damaris loves you, and that you will treat her well. God bless both of you."

In 1893, the little town where they got married had no Salvation Army captain, so they went to the Anglican minister. The rest of David's brothers and sisters were Roman Catholic. He was the lone Protestant in Mary Ann's brood, and Damaris was glad of that.

After his marriage David took up a selection of two hundred acres of virgin bush adjoining Charligrark Lake. With some help from his brothers, he cleared the land and chopped down trees and shaped poles of tough stringybark and bull oak to form the frame and walls of a little bush home.

When the men had the walls in place, Damaris plugged all the cracks and holes with a mortar of yellow clay, smoothing it with her hands so that the interior walls appeared to be plaster lined. For roofing, the men stripped sheets of bark from the stringybark house posts and heated them over a fire of leaves until the bark uncurled and flattened out into strips, three to five feet wide. Heavy poles laid sideways and lengthwise held the bark in place. The inexpensive roofing lasted many years. In fact, that rough bush house with its earth floor and shuttered window holes stood for more than fifty years and, with a few necessary additions, sheltered six children.

Charlie, their firstborn, was 3 years old when his brother David joined the family. He, in turn was 3 when Tom came along. But Tom's birth was a double blessing. He brought a twin sister, Gladys, along with him.

Damaris had her hands more than full. No day was ever long enough for what she had to accomplish. She rose long before daylight to get the kitchen fire going, then stumbled out in the half dark to milk the couple of cows that provided them with all their dairy produce. Next she fed the poultry and collected the eggs before running back to the house to waken the children.

After breakfast she had to fetch the buckets of water from the dam to wash the dishes, and on Mondays to wash the family's clothes. Then she had ironing and cooking and cleaning and, in between, all that, the care of twin babies. If her husband happened to be home, her work was doubled. She had more and bigger meals to cook and more washing to do, and all too often the call was heard, "Demmie, can you come and lend me a hand with this?"

Tom's most vivid memory of his early life concerns his black velvet suit. How his mother ever afforded the luxury of black velvet for her little Tommy-dod's outfit, no one remembers. Most likely it began as a dress belonging to Grandmother Marsh or one of the aunts that Damaris cut down for him. But black velvet it was, with a detachable collar of white lace.

Dressed for a rare visit to town, sixteen miles away, 5-year-old Tommy preened in front of the mirror in his mother's bedroom. Surely, he thought, no little boy ever looked as handsome as he. He blinked his blue eyes at the boy in the mirror and ran a pudgy hand over his shining hair. Then he stroked the soft velvet suit sewn by his mother's loving hands, and for the umpteenth time he adjusted the white lace collar.

As they drove to town in the cart, Tom needed no admonition to "sit still, do." Gladys might twist and wiggle, but he sat like a statue, fearful lest he damage his beautiful suit. All the while mother shopped in town Tom walked behind her, straight and proud, certain that every passer-by looked at him admiringly.

When they reached home after one particular trip to town, the sun had almost set behind the lowering gray clouds that threatened rain. "Change your clothes quickly, Tommy-dod, and come and help me with the cows." Mrs. Crabtree shed her own best dress in record time and grabbed the milk buckets as she ran through the kitchen. "Gladys, you lay the table for supper."

But Tommy, preening again in front of the mirror, could not bear to take off his beloved suit. I'll just remove the lace collar, he thought. It's nearly dark. Mother won't notice my suit.

But she did. Rain began pelting down as he entered the cow yard. Damaris reached for an empty sack hanging on the cowshed wall and draped it over her small helper.

"Oh, you naughty, disobedient boy," she scolded when she looked closely at him. "You didn't change your suit. I'll give you a strapping when we go back to the house."

With that threat hanging over his head, little Tommy raced around in the mud and slush, doing his best to be useful. Surely, if he worked hard, that would placate his mother's anger.

A new calf ran with their big cow, and after his mother finished milking, Tom had to help her lock the calf away from its mother. They succeeded in separating the calf easily enough, but the cow, turned and attacked the person nearest her. And that person happened to be little Tommy-dod in his black velvet suit.

She hooked his velvet pants on her sharp horns and tossed him high into the air to come crashing down, naked into a pile of fresh cow manure.

Quickly the boy scrambled out of her way, but his grief-stricken bellows easily equaled hers. His suit was gone! His beautiful black velvet suit was ripped to pieces!

Frantic with fear, Damaris rushed to aid her bawling son. Tom sensed her anxiety and the possible repeal of her threatened strapping, and howled all the louder.

"There, there, Tommy-dod." She carried him into the kitchen and washed off the mud and muck. His stomach bore long red weals and various scrapes and bruises from the murderous horns, but he was not seriously injured. While she soothed his feelings with kisses and his body with ointment, she pointed out that his disobedience had not only caused the loss of his cherished suit but it could easily have cost his life, as well. If Mrs. Crabtree thought that her son had learned an unforgettable lesson in obedience, she was doomed to disappointment.

Damaris, along with most of the respectable citizens of her day, endeavored to bring her children up in the fear and admonition of the Lord, particularly where it involved the day of worship. Although church services met every four weeks only—the harassed man-of-the-cloth could not manage to conduct services at any of his churches more often than that—Mrs. Crabtree insisted that the family do all the extra work on Saturday.

They had to blacken and shine all the boots, air and press the Sunday clothes, and get the house clean and sparkling— as much as any rough bush house could sparkle. The Sunday roast had to be ready to be warmed in the oven when they returned from church.

Whether it was a church Sunday or not, Damaris always had something special for dinner. Usually it was a roast chicken from their own flock of birds, but sometimes roast mutton if they or the neighbors had killed a sheep recently. People had to share fresh meat. It did not keep long in a water-cooled drip safe. And the family might have baked potatoes and gravy, followed by suet pudding with raisins or bread-and-butter custard.

After midday dinner they visited nearby friends or relatives, or took a walk through the bush. If the day was cold and wet, everyone crouched around the fire and listened while one of the adults read from *The Pilgrim's Progress* or some other suitable book.

Like his father, Abe, David left all the religious matters to his wife. "Men have more to do than read the Bible and sing hymns," he said. Probably the fact that David could neither read nor write fluently had something to do with his aversion to such things. The only schooling any of Mary Ann's children had was the little she taught them, sandwiched in between all her other duties.

"God helps those who help themselves," David retorted when his wife remonstrated with him over his lack of spirituality. "It's all right for you and the kids to observe Sunday, but I've got to work every day to make a living."

Her husband's disinterest pained Damaris, but she comforted herself that he was known for his integrity. Mary Ann had done her work well.

Old Abe Crabtree's grandchildren seemed to be imbued with a double dose of his energy and fire, and poor Damaris found them hard to control. David worked away from home for a large part of the year, leaving her in sole charge of children, animals, and farm. The latter she managed well, but the children caused her a lot of headaches and heartaches.

"They're a real handful," she sighed to Nell, her sister-in-law, who lived close by. "That terrible Crabtree temper smolders like fire in their veins. One never knows when it's going to erupt."

But the children were more high-spirited than bad-tempered. Lively as hares, they frolicked and fought and ran wild and free through the paddocks and bushland. Some of their noisy squabbles nearly drove Damaris distracted.

"You'll never get to heaven if you fight like that," she chided. More often she used the negative approach. "You'll burn in hellfire if you do that," she warned them.

But words alone were not enough. Damaris believed in action, too. She kept three straps that she used for varying offenses.

The first one was the crupper. A rolled leather contraption that went under a horse's tail and helped to hold the riding saddle in place. When not in use on the horse, it hung on a nail outside the back door.

She employed the crupper for the worst offenders. It hurt like fury. An application of it to a boy's backside almost certainly brought results.

Next came the razor strop, a double-leather device on which David sharpened his razor. The strop was about two or three inches across and left a wide red welt around a boy's legs when wielded expertly.

Last was a long, narrow leather strap from a piece of broken harness. It did not hurt nearly as much as the first two, and she reserved it for light offenses, or for chastising Gladys, the only girl in the family.

Those straps, all three of them, were the bane of the Crabtree children's lives.

"Why don't we play a trick on Mother," David Junior suggested to his brother Tom one evening. "She's down in the cow yard and won't be back until the milking's done."

They posted Gladys at the corner of the house to keep watch, and then the two boys dragged a ladder into the kitchen. Tom, being the smaller, climbed to the top, and David handed up hammer and nails and the hated straps. One by one Tom nailed them to the roof beam that extended across the twenty-foot-wide kitchen.

Hardly had they replaced the ladder when their lookout hissed, "Here she comes!"

Immediately the two boys began a sham fight. They rolled over and over on the hard earth floor, biting and yelling and punching—to all appearances locked in mortal combat.

"Oh, you dreadful boys!" Damaris tramped in and dumped her milk-buckets near the kitchen stove. "You're always fighting. Stop it. Stop it right now!"

The boys ignored her. The scuffles and yells showed no sign of abating, so she reached for the light harness strap. It was not there.

She felt for the razor strop that always hung on a nail behind the kitchen door. It had also vanished.

With an exasperated sigh Mother stepped outside to where the horse's harness hung on wooden pegs driven into the back wall of the hut. But, the crupper was missing, too. For a split second she stared unbelievingly at the empty space.

The boys stopped their sham fight and breathlessly waited her reaction. Suddenly she burst out laughing. Gladys laughed, too, and the boys joined in. For several minutes they all hugged their mother, and she declared that it was a fine joke. But all the same, once she wiped her eyes with the corner of her apron, they had to climb up to the rafters, take down the straps, and restore them to their rightful places.

"Why don't you bawl like I do?" David asked his brother Tom one day. "They don't hit half so hard or for half as long if you cry and yell and make a fuss." Nearly four years older than Tom, he was much more worldlywise.

But Tom was too proud or too stubborn to cry. He took his punishments tight-lipped and dry-eyed—and suffered for it. His father hated his proud, rebellious son, and vowed to break his spirit or kill him in the attempt.

One blazing hot day when Tom was 10 years old, his father sent him and younger brother Willie to collect the mail. "Come straight back home," he warned. "Don't loiter around the lake. There's plenty of work for you here."

Collecting the mail entailed a long walk in the pitiless sun, made all the more unbearable by the close proximity of the beckoning blue water. Several times the boys waded in to cool their bare feet and gulp a drink from their cupped hands.

They collected the mail, and on their way back they met Joe and Bill, two neighbor boys, splashing around in the shallows. "Come on in," they invited. "The water's great on a day like this."

"We can't," Tom explained regretfully. "Dad said to hurry back with the mail."

"Aw, come on." Joe was older and most persuasive. "Your Dad wont' mind if you cool off for a few minutes." When Tom and Will still hesitated, he added, "We'll go back with you and make it all right with him."

With such assurance, the Crabtree boys stripped off their ragged shirts and trousers and rushed in. The water cooled their burning skin and washed the dust from their sandy hair. For half an hour the four boys frolicked and swam as carefree as the tadpoles they disturbed in the reedy marshes.

Then Tom and Will decided that they had better hurry home, but Joe and Bill had second thoughts. "You go on home," Joe directed nonchalantly. "Your dad won't say anything. We gotta get back now and do our own chores."

With hearts turned to stone the Crabtree boys realized what this refusal would mean. Dread dogged their lagging footsteps and gave their father's temper more time to boil.

"You give him the mail," Tom directed his younger brother. Will was their father's favorite. He might be able to save the situation.

Will handed him the mail, and one look at the boy's ruffled, still damp hair confirmed his father's suspicions. "You went into the lake when I told you not to!" he roared.

"Joe and Bill were there," his son said trembling.

At that, Tom, listening behind the shed, bolted into the house in search of his mother. But her presence could not save him. Like a tornado his father whirled into the house after him.

"Where's that boy?" His furious eyes meant business. "Why did you disobey me?"

He dragged Tom out into the yard and boxed his ears. But that wasn't enough. In his rage he looked around for a weapon, and his eyes fell on the steel-handled whip sticking out of its holder on the side of the buggy.

"I'll teach you to do as you're told." Tom's father seized the whip and flogged him with the steel handle until he fell unconscious at his feet.

Tom never knew how much time elapsed, but when he came to, his father had gone, and he was lying in the shade of a laurel tree with his mother's tears falling like warm rain on his face.

"Mother," he groaned, "as soon as I'm old enough, I'm going to leave home and never come back."

She wept even harder. "Lie still," she sobbed, then mopped her eyes with the folds of her calico apron. "Lie still, while I get some ointment.

She fetched a basin of hot water, red with Condy's* and bathed the tattered shirt off his back. Then she applied ointment to the crisscrossed welts and bound up his body with a torn-up sheet. "It'll be better soon," she comforted him, and Tom tasted her salty tears on his lips as she kissed him.

Tom was not the only one who suffered. When something aroused their father's temper, he was even wilder than old Abe.

One morning Tom heard shouting and ran outside to see Charlie racing across the paddocks with their father after him. Tom shivered. He had no idea what his brother had done—or not done—but it was clear that he was in for it if their father caught him.

The noise attracted their mother's attention, and she came out of the house too. Together she and Tom watched helplessly as Charlie dashed, fully clothed, into the lake, and frantically swam out of his father's reach.

It was beneath his father's dignity to take off his boots and go in after the boy. Instead, cursing and threatening at the top of his voice, he mounted his horse and whipped the animal into the water.

Seeing him coming, Charlie doubled back and swam to shore. Shaking with cold and fear he stumbled over the uneven ground toward the house. But Mr. Crabtree, on horseback, easily caught up with him and cut off his retreat.

Speechless with fury, the father slid off his horse and wrenched a paling from the rickety fence. Grabbing his shrinking son by the arm, he struck him with the board. Around they went in circles, Charlie trying to tear himself from his father's grasp, the father whacking him at every turn.

Finally David Crabtree fell to the ground, too giddy to continue the punishment, and a sobbing boy escaped and hid in the haystack until his father cooled down.

Mercifully for the children, Mr. Crabtree spent much of his time away classing wool. He worked at his profession to earn the cash that the family needed, and Damaris shouldered the responsibility of raising the six children—another boy, Keith, was now the youngest—and carving a farm out of the

*Permanganate of potash, usually called Condy's crystals.

untamed bush.

She could wield an ax nearly as well as a man. As soon as the boys were old enough, she took them out into the bush with her and taught them how to ringbark trees with their little tomahawks. The process prevented the life-giving sap from rising up the tree trunks, and the tree eventually died. A year or two after the ringbarking, they returned and she showed them how to kindle brush fires and burn the now dead and dry trees.

No one cared about the wanton waste of good timber. Australia in those days was lavish in its natural wealth. Little wonder that the sun-starved English immigrants still flocking to the new land thought that they had discovered paradise. Rich soil, abundant rainfall, timber for the taking—Australia offered them everything they needed. It was all there, but it took cruel, backbreaking toil to wrest from the earth its bounties.

Mrs. Crabtree knew how to work, and she saw to it that her children did their share. Not one of them grew up to be lazy.

Little by little their fortunes improved with the passing years. Their few sheep grew into a sizable flock. With his knowledge of wool and breeding, Mr. Crabtree had the best sheep obtainable. His yearly wool clip, though small, was valuable.

Two or three cows supplied the family with liberal quantities of milk and cheese, and cream for butter. Chickens, turkeys, ducks, and geese kept the old farm lively with their sounds.

They sowed every piece of cleared land with barley or oats as feed for the stock, and as they grew older, the boys cleared more land and planted it with wheat to sell.

They began breeding horses, too. From one of his trips David brought home an old mare named Linda. Linda was in foal and everyone in the family excitedly awaited the big event.

Grandmother Marsh died on September 26, 1909. Doubtless her daughter Damaris mourned for her, but the grandchildren didn't. That same day Linda had her foal, and that event crowded all other thoughts out of their young minds. They named it Minnie, and chattered excitedly about the fine team of horses they would eventually have when her children and grandchildren grew up.

Horses were something the Crabtree children coveted. The nearest school was six miles away over the rough bush trail that passed for a road. For a long time the older boys and Gladys had traveled to school with Joe and Bill in the neighbor's springless cart, pulled by gallant old Mick.

But one afternoon, coming home from school with half a dozen children tumbling and playing in the wooden cart, old Mick fell and the cart shaft broke. The horse struggled to his feet and kicked himself free of the hampering harness, but in the effort the jagged end of the broken shaft drove into his belly. When he finally pushed himself upright, his intestines bulged out of the bloody gash.

"Quick! Go and get Dad!" Joe clambered out of the cart and dashed off up the track, while the horrified younger children stared tearfully at the twitching horse. In a short time the neighbor rode up and with a well-aimed shot put the poor animal out of his misery.

From then on the children had to walk to and from school. In winter they stumbled along the mist-veiled, frosty trail, with cold feet and chattering teeth. In summer they panted and sweated as they trudged the dusty, drought-cracked earth.

Mrs. Crabtree insisted that her boys and girl must all attend school. Moreover, while most of the other children in the district went barefoot, she somehow managed to provide hers with stout leather boots and woolen socks. Every night she insisted that they blacken their boots and place them beside their beds, and in the morning she proudly saw her family off to school with clean clothes and shiny footwear.

It puzzled her, though, that while the boys' shirts and trousers showed obvious signs of wear and tear their boots never appeared muddied or scraped after their long hike.

"I simply can't understand it," she commented to Aunt Nell. "Those children are so light on boots. They grow out of them before the leather shows any signs of wear."

Some time passed before she discovered that as soon as

they left the farm behind, the children took off their heavy leather boots and hid them in a culvert, ready to collect and don on the homeward journey. They walked faster without boots. Years of running barefoot around the farm had made the soles of their feet as tough as leather. They trod on the sharpest stones and prickliest thistles and scarcely felt them.

The miles seemed endless, but there was much to see and hear on the way to school: toadstools in the moist brown leafmold, bellbirds clinking, and kookaburras laughing with raucous glee. Sometimes a wallaby balanced on hind legs and tail, nibbling at succulent grass shoots.

One morning Charlie made a new discovery, and his excited shout brought the others running. "Hey, look at this!" He pointed to dingo tracks in the dust.

"I wonder which way he went?"

Quiet as mice, they followed the tracks until they disappeared on the bank of a narrow creek. "No hope of seeing him now." Charlie shrugged and led the way back to the road.

Tom lingered behind, straining to see into the bushes on the other side. Suddenly the muddy bank gave away and the startled 7-year-old plunged into the shallow stream.

"Help!" he screamed, and scrambled out, cold and dripping. There was no question of returning home. Despite the fact that he was soaked, the boy knew that he must go on to school. Miserably he plodded the last two miles and presented his shivering self, along with the other pupils, at the one-roomed schoolhouse.

"Oh, dearie me." Young Miss Argyle threw her hands up when she saw the state of his clothes and his chattering teeth. "This will never do. Charlie, you and Joe light the fire. Quickly now. You other boys bring in more wood. Mary, drag my big chair up in front of the fire."

While the children scurried to obey, Miss Argyle peeled off Tom's sodden clothes and wrapped him in a towel. "There." She sat him in the chair and tucked her own coat around him for extra warmth. "You'll have to stay right there until your clothes dry, Tommy."

He nodded, and his adoring eyes watched her every move as she spread his clothes out over a second chair and called the other children inside to begin the day's lessons.

Every time Miss Argyl turned her back, the children winked and pointed at Tom and mouthed, "Little Tommy, teacher's pet." But he didn't mind. His heart felt warm as well as his body. He had seldom experienced special attention, and he liked it.

It was no secret that Tom loved his teacher.

With the tip of his protruding tongue testifying to the intensity of his concentration, his slate pencil squeaked across his smeary slate as he labored over his pothooks.* Or he industriously rattled the colored beads on his abacus back and forth—all to earn a quick pat on his sandy head and Miss Argyl's "Good work, Tommy."

On Monday and Friday afternoons the boys and girls fetched spades and hoes and watering cans out of the school's shed, and under Miss Argyl's direction they weeded and watered their individual gardenplots. Some of the children already had a well-developed sense of thrift—they grew vegetables. Others planted flowers.

"Come here, Tommy; you can help me." Tom's little heart leaped as his teacher singled him out. "We'll plant chrysanthemums in this bed alongside the steps."

Chrysanthemums. Tom hadn't the slightest idea what they were, but the word sounded soft and lovely the way she said it. Chrysanthemums. He tried it himself, under his breath. Over and over like a whispered song: "Chrysanthemums. Chrysanthemums."

Miss Argyle handed him the seeds and explained that chrysanthemums were flowers. "Beautiful flowers, Tom. Hardy, too. I'm sure they'll grow well in this soil."

On Tuesday morning the upper grades had a spelling lesson, and Miss Argyle wrote on the blackboard the names of the seeds they had planted: "LETTUCE, SPINACH, CUCUMBER," they intoned after her. "PANSIES, PHLOX, CHRYSANTHEMUMS."

---

*Marks used in teaching writing.

Tom, in first grade, was supposed to be reading his primer, but he couldn't tear his eyes away from the blackboard. Chrysanthemums. What a long word it was. Nevertheless, he idolized Miss Argyle to such an extent that "chrysanthemums" became the first long word he learned to spell.

Tom's love for his teacher influenced him a lot, but it didn't make him perfect. While he tried to be good at school and please her, he didn't always succeed. Then, just as if she were an ordinary mortal like his mother, Miss Argyle whaled into him with strap or cane.

Tom bore no grudges. In fact, the older he grew, the harder he tried. By the time he had graduated from slate to lead pencil to pen and ink, he had developed a callus on the top joint of his second finger on the right hand where the steel-nibbed pen bit in. Writing had to be copybook perfect. Nothing less would please his teacher.

A wall map of the world, a tables chart, and a cane were the only teaching aids the little bush school boasted. Nevertheless Miss Argyle's ingenuity made learning a pleasure, and most of her pupils acquitted themselves well in the government examinations that marked the end of their primary school training.

Twelve miles a day was a lot of walking—far too much for 7- and 8-year old legs. By the time little brother, Keith Crabtree, was ready for school, the authorities recognized it. Or was it because the old Broughton place had been sold and the new owner had a large family of boys?

Whatever the influencing factor, the government opened a part-time school only a quarter of a mile from the Crabtree farm. It met in Mr. Broughton's old office, the same room where Hopping Abe had told the gentleman farmer that he needn't go to hell now.

Education was not the only thing that came a bit rough and ready in the first decades of the twentieth century. Bush doctoring was a science all its own.

Isolated farmers kept a stock of home remedies for ailments affecting man or beast. Iodine, Condy's and castor oil were as essential household items as flour, sugar, and tea.

Coughs and colds, cuts and bruises; earache, stomach-ache, and toothache; croup and fever and diarrhea; every bush man and woman had his or her favorite remedies for them. Only when accidents or serious disease struck did those sturdy pioneers seek outside help.

With five active, accident-prone boys in the family, Mrs. Crabtree was sometimes at her wits' end to know how to deal with their mishaps.

One such occasion, when Charlie was 12 and David Junior was nearly 9, proved to be beyond her meager knowledge. The two boys were playing one of their rough-and-tumble games in the barn. Charlie, showing off in front of his younger brother, climbed up the wall of one of the horse stalls. On his way down again, he slipped and caught his knee on a projecting stub of one of the rough-hewn sapling posts. The branch was less than an inch thick, but it drove right in under his kneecap and broke off.

The boy yelled with pain and fright, and his younger brother ran shouting for help. Both parents came running, but it was something that neither of them could handle. "Run and call Mrs. Wong. Tell her to come quickly."

Old Dr. Fairburn, the alcoholic, had died many years ago, but Mrs. Wong, a Chinese woman of unknown age, had somehow inherited his reputation and some of his instruments.

Fear lent wings to David's bare feet, and while he raced off in the direction of Mrs. Wong's humble abode, the adults carried Charlie into the kitchen.

Quickly David returned with the old woman. While Mr. Crabtree and Uncle Francis held Charlie still on a wooden chair, Mrs. Wong picked up a cutthroat razor. With one swift stroke she opened Charlie's knee.

The room exploded with yelling and screaming. Mr. Crabtree shouted at Charlie to be still, the boy's mother hid her face, and the other children looked on in terrified fascination. Only Uncle Francis remained calm. He hung onto Charlie's leg and somehow kept it still while Mrs. Wong used Dr. Fairburn's tweezers to pick a two-inch splinter out of the knee. Then she poured yellow iodoform into the wound, bound the knee with strips of old sheets, and ordered him to bed for two weeks.

At the end of the fortnight Charlie was up and around, and his knee was as good as new.

Some time later Tom had firsthand experience of Mrs. Wong's expertise. One of the hens insisted on laying her eggs in the hayloft. His mother knew they were there, and apparently wanting the hen to hatch her chicks in peace, she forbade the children to play in the loft.

But, when anyone told Tom not to do something, that became the thing that he wanted most to do.

One afternoon, while his mother and the rest of the family were occupied elsewhere, he climbed up the narrow ladder into the hayloft and searched for the nest. "I know it's here somewhere," he muttered. Ignoring the indignant squawking of the disturbed hen, he shuffled across the hay-littered floor until he found the hidden eggs.

"Aha!" he dropped to his knees. But his triumphant cry changed to a yelp of pain as the jagged edge of a broken bottle gashed his left leg just below the knee.

Blood streamed from the cut as Tom slid down the ladder and headed for the stable. Why the stable, he did not know, but he had to go somewhere well away from his mother and the punishment he knew his disobedience merited.

Hurriedly poking around in the stable, Tom found the sleeve of an old shirt lying in a stall. Quickly he picked it up and shook out the dirt and manure. With Mrs. Wong's treatment of Charlie in mind, he washed the blood off in the horse trough, and bound the filthy rag tightly around his knee. With his trouser leg pulled well down to cover the "bandage," Tom managed to hide all evidence of the accident.

His leg pained, but he could stand the hurt . . . anything so long as his mother did not find out where he'd been.

Unfortunately for Tom, as the days passed the pain increased. His leg stiffened and he limped as he walked.

Eventually his mother noticed his lameness, and despite his protests, she insisted on inspecting his leg.

She nearly fainted at what she saw. Then she immediately summoned Mrs. Wong. Her round, oriental face remained impassive, but she went to work.

While Tom gritted his teeth and clenched his fists to keep from crying out, she cleaned his wound with hot water and poured in generous quantities of iodoform powder. Then she bandaged his leg and ordered him to bed for two weeks.

By some miracle he escaped tetanus, and, after nearly driving his mother mad during his two weeks of enforced inactivity, he got up and raced around as wild as ever.

When he was old enough to reason things out, Tom recognized his good fortune in having Mrs. Wong treat him, and not old Dr. Mackaullie. Dr. Mackaullie was another of the bush doctors who had left the cities for various reasons and eked a precarious living out of the ills and accidents of the isolated country folk.

Tom had never seen Dr. Mackaullie. He did not even know whether the man was dead by now. But he often saw Mr. Bamfield, one of Mackaullie's patients, and he shuddered as he recalled the oft-heard story.

One day Mr. Bamfield, of Brinkallert station, had become involved in a discussion on hunting. Somehow, during the more than animated conversation, Mr. Bamfield had waved his gun around and accidentally shot himself in the knee.

Fortunately, or unfortunately, Dr. Mack, who had also imbibed far too freely, arrived on the scene. "Take y' breeches off, Bam," he said thickly. "I'll have to get that bullet out."

Mr. Bamfield complied and the doctor set to work, probing the injured leg without success. He tried again. And yet again. Blood flowed as freely as the profanities pouring from Mr. Bamfield's suffering lips.

At last Dr. Mack straightened his back and stared owlishly at his patient. "I'm afraid I'll have to take your leg off, Bam. There's nothing else for it. You'll die if I don't get that piece of lead out."

Either Mr. Bamfield was too drunk or in too much pain to protest, and preparation went ahead for the amputation. Willing hands cleared the junk off the big kitchen table. More hands hoisted Mr. Bamfield up onto it. His friends dosed him with Brandy until he fell back senseless.

Then Dr. Mack took a nip or two to settle his nerves and, under the awed eyes of his half tipsy audience, set to work.

There was no one there to tie off veins or stanch the blood, and it was with some difficulty that Dr. Mack managed to amputate the leg. Finally he finished and as he lifted the severed limb to throw it into the waiting bucket, the bullet clinked onto the floor.

Staring at it, Dr. Mack shook his head stupidly. "It couldn't a' been in very far at all," he muttered.

Before the accident Mr. Bamfield, so the story went, had operated two large sheep stations and was well on the way to becoming a wealthy man. But when he lost his leg that all changed. He could not adequately care for his flocks and cattle, nor sow his fields with grain. His payments lagged and the banks foreclosed on his mortgage. Eventually he lost his farms.

Disappointed, Mrs. Bamfield also took to drink. As they grew up, the Bamfield sons did likewise.

When Tom was a little boy Pegleg Bamfield drove around in a shabby old buggy drawn by an ancient horse, a living testimony, if anyone had heeded it, to the results of alcohol.

Sometimes Damaris found it hard to discipline her unruly tribe, and when lectures and punishments failed, she resorted to threats of the unknown. In May, 1910, Halley's comet became visible in the night sky. She used its appearance to strike terror into her boys.

"If that comet's tail touches the earth, it will be the end of the world," she solemnly assured them. "Watch out for it. If you keep on with your naughtiness, you'll be burned up with the rest of the wicked. You'd better mend your ways, you boys."

Outwardly her sons scoffed at her notion, but inwardly they had misgivings. Tom, at least, kept a sharp eye on the comet as he drove the cows home each night. He trudged across the paddocks with his head thrown back so that he could see the sky.

Surely, he thought, as he stumbled over the clods and tussocks, its great long tail was nearing the earth. Over there behind the hill it must be dragging close to the ground. It *must* be going to touch soon. If not tonight, then tomorrow, or maybe the next night.

"Come along, dreamer. It's not here yet." Tom jumped at the sound of his brother David's voice out of the gloom. Neither boy said anything more, but Tom realized that his older brother was putting on a bold front. Undoubtedly, he too was more worried about their mother's predictions than he'd cared to admit.

The strain of being good was hard to bear, and Tom was a mightily relieved 10-year-old when finally the great comet disappeared into space and he could look up at the stars without his heart skipping a beat.

On one occasion, when the boys' quarrels and fist fights had been more violent than usual, their mother declared that she had had enough. "I'm going to drown myself," she said, then jammed her faded sunbonnet onto her graying hair. "You children can do as you like once I'm gone."

Stunned silence greeted her announcement. The group watched open-mouthed as she banged the kitchen door behind her and marched off down the paddock.

Then Will, the second youngest, spoke. "Let's go and watch her do it." As one, the six of them scurried across the yard and followed her across the fields. They found her sitting on a fallen log beside the dam, crying her heart out.

Of course, her grief touched their hearts and they promised to be good. But she was adamant. She had heard all that many times before. Now she'd had enough—it was the end.

The children had to literally force her back to the house. The big boys took her arms, and with the younger ones pushing behind her legs, they goose-stepped her home again.

For a while—all too short a while—they kept their promise. Then the four older boys fashioned bows and arrows for themselves and took sides for a game of Indians—David and Tom against Charlie and Will.

The battle raged back and forth until, whooping and shrieking, David and Tom drove Charlie and Will to take refuge in the house. The latter slammed the kitchen door and felt safe. But the roughwood door had a knothole and David sent an arrow through the knothole just at the moment that Charlie put his eye to it to see what was going on.

"Ouch! You've hit me! You've killed me!" he bellowed. "Let me out."

Frightened by what they'd done, the victors opened the door, and Charlie rushed out and grabbed David. "You've hit my eye!" he bawled. "I'll kill you."

Now it was David's turn to yell. "Help! He's killing me! Charlie's killing me!"

All the fun went out of the game. Murder glinted in the older boy's eyes, and Tom and Will ran for their lives.

Their mother did too. From away down at Aunt Nell's house she heard the shouting. "They're up to something——" She cut her visit short and tore home.

"Oh, you terrible boys! Oh, you wicked boys! You promised me—oh, what shall I do?" Again she dissolved into tears.

By the time Tom and Will sneaked back into the kitchen, the two combatants were on their knees promising their mother that it would never happen again. Peace reigned, at least for the duration of Charlie's black eye. It sobered even the heedless Crabtree boys when Damaris pointed out that if the arrow had struck a fraction to the left, it might have blinded their big brother.

The boys quarreled and fought almost constantly among themselves, but let a stranger attack one of the brothers and the other four descended upon him in a howling fury. One time, in Will's defense, Tom wrestled another boy into a hole and furiously filled earth in on top of him.

"Don't you dare touch my brother!" he shouted as the

terrified lad scrabbled and clawed his way out of the hole. "I'll pile rocks on top of you next time."

Damaris tried to instill some religion into her unruly brood, though she did not tuck each one into bed with a goodnight kiss and a bedtime story. No, indeed. Life was too hard, and she was far too busy for that. But as each little one came along she taught him to say his prayers.

Every morning, as they grew older, she prayed with her family before they set off for school. Sometimes, on wet Sundays, she read to them from her Salvation Army books, or taught them songs and stories she had learned long ago in her own Sunday school days.

Mr. Crabtree took no interest in her religious exercises, but once a month, if he was at home, the whole family piled into the springless farm cart and went to church. It was as often as the itinerant Anglican minister opened up the little wooden church at Booroopki. Although she was not Anglican, nothing short of an earthquake kept Damaris home.

The drive to church over the rutted roads was less than pleasant. The parents and whichever child was youngest at the time sat on a rug-covered board across the front of the cart. Cushioned with hay, the other children sat in the bed, facing inward, their backs scraping against the cart's wooden sides and their legs stuck stiffly out in front of them.

They did their best to please their mother and keep their Sunday clothes clean and presentable. No one attempted any larks or pranks—not with father, whip in hand, at such close proximity. Even too-loud talking risked their father's displeasure. All the same, the children gladly endured the journey for the sake of the outing.

True, most of the young people they met at church were the same ones they saw at school all week. But on Sundays they looked different. The boys all wore squeaky leather boots and had their hair neatly combed and plastered down with heavy oil or axle grease. The girls preened in ruffled dresses, and ribbons or bows adorned their frizzed or ringletted hair.

Miss Argyle looked splendid in her high-buttoned boots

and white frilled blouse, with a large cameo brooch pinned at her throat. Tom thought she stood out like a princess among the farmwives in their plain black alpacas.

The latter had work-worn hands in much-mended gloves and fumbled awkwardly with the brollies that shaded them from the blistering noonday sun or protected them from showers.

The sermon, like the long drive, the children tolerated for the sake of the more pleasant aspects of church. After the minister shook hands at the door, the dismissed congregation magically resolved into groups. The men made a beeline for the horses and vehicles, and their talk of crops, prices, flocks, and herds was far from "Sabbathy."

The women opened their brollies and peeled off their gloves and comfortably set out to catch up on the latest news. The youths and girls stood around in awkward groups, ogling and giggling, none daring to make a move in front of their elders. They reserved flirting strictly for the rare bush picnics and the even more rare barn dances.

The younger children disappeared behind the church, intent on activities of their own. The babies and toddlers squalled or raced underfoot and spoiled everyone's concentration, until finally one of the deacons unhitched his horse and bawled, "Come on, Mother. It's time we got going." Then the company reluctantly broke up and drove the long road home for Sunday dinner.

Religious doctrines did not figure largely in their lives, and it somewhat shocked Tom when he overheard his mother tell Aunt Nell that Christians went to church on the wrong day.

"You know," she said, "we keep the wrong day holy. Saturday is the Sabbath, but the Jews are the only ones who observe it."

The boy pricked up his ears and heard his aunt demand, "Who told you that?"

"When I was a little girl, my schoolteacher, Mr. Caleb, said so. He's right. I looked on a calendar. Sunday is the *first* day of the week. The commandment says, 'The *seventh* day is the sabbath of the Lord thy God.' "

Tom wandered off to play then, but that scrap of information lay dormant in his mind for more than fourteen years.

THE UNTAMABLE TOM

As the boys grew older their quarrels lost nothing in frequency, and gained a great deal in ferocity.

One morning it was Tom's turn to bring in the firewood. As he staggered in with each load and stacked it by the big kitchen fireplace he noticed his older brother, David, busily carving something into the rough wooden post at the side of the fireplace.

At first Tom did not pay much attention to what his brother was doing. One or another of them often whittled or sharpened his clasp knife on the solid wood posts. Besides, every time he entered the kitchen, his brother nonchalantly stepped to one side so that he stood directly in front of his handiwork.

Presently Tom deposited the last armload of firewood on the stack, brushed his sleeves, and idly turned to see what so absorbed David's attention. The brother tried to cover the carving with his left hand, but he was too late. Tom saw the name "LIZZIE" scored deep into the wood.

Lizzie was one of the girls at school. He disliked her because she delighted in persuading the other boys to hold him down while she kissed him.* Why was David carving *her* name into their fireplace? A sudden suspicion seized him, and he dragged his brother's left hand aside. Sure enough, David had carved "TOM," a crude heart shape, and then "LIZZIE."

"You!" Howling with rage, Tom snatched one of the three-pronged deer-horn-handled forks from the breakfast table. "You—you—wretch!" He drove it with all his might into his brother's back.

With a roar of pain, David rushed to the other end of the long room where their mother was slicing bread.

---

* Years later he met her in town. She had grown into an attractive young woman, and he offered to kiss *her* then. But she would have none of it.

"Mum! Mum!" he yelped. "Tom——"

As he reached her side the fork clattered onto the floor. David swooped it up and charged for his brother. But Damaris rushed between them. With Solomonic justice she decreed that David must scrape and smooth the wood until he had obliterated every vestige of his inscription. To keep Tom out of the way while he did it, she sent him down to the dairy to help Gladys churn the milk.

One particular weekend, when Tom was about 12 years old, his mother gave him permission to go along with Joe and Bill, the neighbor boys, to an important football match in a neighboring town.

But just before he was due to leave she discovered that he had not chopped the firewood or polished the boots for Sunday. That put the situation in a different light. They were his Saturday chores, and he knew it. Each of the other children had jobs to do. Of course he could not go to a football match if he had not finished his work.

Tom did not answer his mother. Setting his jaw stubbornly, he picked up the ax. But instead of chopping firewood, he coaxed Gladys, his twin, to drop his boots and best clothes out of the bedroom window. In no time at all he had changed in the barn and raced across the fields to his rendezvous with Joe and Bill.

Once in their smart new gig, bumping along behind the steady gray mare, Tom tried to join in the excited chatter and laughter of the other lads. But something was wrong. Every turn of the iron-shod wooden wheels seemed to creak, "Will you—disobey mother—like this?"

And instead of the gray mare's hoofs going *clip-clop, clip-clop,* as they usually did, they seemed to Tom to be saying, "Will you? Will you?"

He squirmed miserably. Nothing so gnaws into a boy's vitals as a guilty conscience. Finally Joe, the older boy, noticed that something was wrong and demanded to know what it was. Almost eagerly, Tom confessed.

To his surprise, instead of congratulating him on his

smartness, Joe shook his head. "You'd better go back home, Tom. S'pose something happened on our way to the football match and you got killed. Then what?"

Bill nodded in equally solemn agreement. They both looked at him as if his fate were already sealed.

He needed no further urging. Joe pulled the gray mare to a halt, and Tom clambered down and trudged the long miles back home to face his mother and his well-deserved punishment.

But she did not discipline him. Stern-faced, she listened to his confession and then directed him to take off his best clothes and hurry on with his chores. As he turned to obey, he thought he saw tears in her eyes.

Tom polished the family boots as he had never done them before. Then he chopped a huge pile of firewood and stacked it by the kitchen stove. That night his mother prepared his favorite foods, mutton stew and dumplings, with raspberry-jam roll and clotted cream for dessert. The boy said nothing, but he smiled across the table at his mother, and she smiled back, and he knew how the prodigal son must have felt when he returned from a far country.

About this time 15-year-old David began to fancy himself a man of the world. He did an adult's work on the farm, and he reasoned that an occasional secret smoke down behind the hay shed was legitimate, considering his deep voice and sprouting whiskers. Also he took up swearing. But he made sure that no brothers or sister were around to report on him. A couple of times, though, Tom heard him and threatened to tell their mother.

David pleaded with him not to, offering Tom anything he wanted if only he would keep silent about it to their mother.

Damaris equated swearing with the unpardonable sin. She hated tobacco and liquor, too, but somehow she accepted them as lusts of the flesh to which all men succumbed. But swearing was different—particularly any oath that took God's name in vain.

Tom promised not to tell, but he found it a most profitable

form of blackmail. If his brother displeased him, he only had to mouth the words "I'll tell Mother," and David fell into line with his wishes.

The day he received his Merit Certificate Tom's schooling ended. He had gone as high as he could go at the local school. Both Miss Argyle and his current girlfriend pleaded with him to continue.

"You could earn a scholarship, Tom. Go to Adelaide and study to become a teacher."

But he shook his head. Only those few who chose to follow one of the professions—medicine, law, or teaching—followed the hard road to higher learning. He had the wanderlust and wanted to get out and carve a life for himself. Besides, there was still his father. Tom couldn't leave home quickly enough.

True to his vow of earlier years, 14-year-old Tom went as far away from home as he could, accepting a job on a cattle station twenty miles from Mount Gambier in South Australia. He butchered cattle for the nearby village of Kalongadoo, a task that brought him in touch with a lot of people. Since he liked them and they liked him, he would have been happy to continue butchering for as long as he lived. But the guns of World War I boomed across Europe. Britain needed help from her far-flung colonies. Charlie and David Crabtree answered the call, which left Mr. Crabtree with no one to help him manage the farm. He sent for Tom, and being legally under age, the youth had to return.

However, it soon became apparent that the two could never work together, and the father arranged for Tom to labor for their new neighbor, Harry Bullins.

Harry was the worst kind of man—he bullied his wife and his children. His horses shied away from him, and his dogs cringed at the sound of his curses. He expected Tom to do the work of three men.

"Ya can't work 'orses without swearin' at 'em," he told Tom. "They don't unnerstan' anythin' but cusses."

Cursing, like smoking and drinking, appeared to Tom as hallmarks of approaching manhood. He readily became proficient in the art of swearing at the plow horses.

Although Tom worked from dawn till dusk six days a week, he could not satisfy Harry. Mr. Bullins growled and blamed him for everything that went wrong. One morning Harry cursed Tom for being a few minutes late with the milking, and the boy quit on the spot.

Before his father had time to find out and vent his anger, Tom went to work for Mr. Carver. All the able-bodied young men had gone off to war and jobs were easy to come by. But Carver proved to be a worse boss than Bullins had been, and Tom slaved from before cold dawn until far into the still, dark night.

The climax came one bitter winter day when the exhausted boy slept in until 7:00 A.M. The previous day the weather prophets had predicted rain, so Carver kept the lad up until two in the morning, cutting and carting chaff from his other farm, five miles distant. When at last he fell into bed Tom slept like one dead.

But the older man rose at the usual hour. In a towering rage he stamped out to where his hired hand lived in a little room at the back of the farmhouse.

"Get up, lazybones!" he roared. "What sort of time is this? Why aren't you out feeding the horses?"

Tom dragged his sleep-heavy eyes open. "What sort of time was it when I got to bed?" he retorted.

Mr. Carver's face reddened as if he was about to have apoplexy. "I won't stand any nonsense from you," he flared. "You can come and get your pay."

"All right." Tom rolled out of bed and reached for his boots. Quickly he wrapped his few possessions up in his blanket and presented himself at Carver's office for his pay.

"Aw, go and feed the horses, Tom." The man had visibly cooled.

"No. I want my pay."

"Go and have your breakfast. We can talk——"

"No, I won't eat another mouthful of your maggotty meat and filthy bread. Give me my pay. I'm going home for a decent feed."

"You cheeky young hound." His hands trembled with rage, and he railed at Tom for at least ten minutes before scrawling out a check for four pounds and pushing it across the table to Tom.

"What's this for?"

"That's your wages. I can't afford to pay you any more than that."

"Four pounds for a whole month's work, and slaving at that! Well, if you're that poor, Mr. Carver, I'll make you a present of the four pounds." Disdainfully he flicked the check in the man's direction and headed for the door.

When Tom reached home and told his father what had happened, it produced another fireworks display. But Tom was too big to thrash now. Mr. Crabtree had to content himself with riding over to Carver to apologize on his son's behalf and collect his pay—and he kept the money, every penny of it.

Tom's next job involved picking grapes at Mildura. He was 16 now, and it was the easiest thing he had done in his life. Although prepared to work for the entire grape-picking season, he ran afoul of another youth—the boss's favorite—and once more he found himself out of a job.

After that Tom sat down and did some serious thinking. There were not many good jobs around, and he was tired of slaving for some mercenary skinflint in search of cheap labor.

"It's better for me if I work for myself," he decided. So, young as he was, he took up contract work, grubbing out trees and clearing land for a new road. When that ended he did odd jobs for old, wrinkled Mrs. Molloy, now retired from the hotel where Abe had once crawled for refuge.

"Old Abe's grandson are ye, ye spalpeen?"* she crowed delightedly. "I mind well the night he came knockin' at our door. I was only young, newly married 'n all; 'n I had charge of the hotel while me husband was away. Oh, what a man that granddaddy of yours was——" The old woman proceeded to fill Tom's mouth with cake and his ears with tales of wild Abe's doings and sayings.

———
* Rascal.

LFIHV-6

After finishing Mrs. Molloy's odd jobs, Tom found work on a station. There he learned to rope wild horses and to break them in for riding and farmwork. He learned something else, too. Mixing with rough boundary riders and drovers—some of them lawless men—taught him to say No to alcohol.

Apart from the pain it would bring his mother if he took up drink, Tom saw that alcohol only used up hard-earned money and left a fellow no better off.

"Not for me," he'd say when the men passed the rum bottle around. "I'm saving up to get married." That sally always brought forth a roar of laughter, but the older men left him alone and concentrated on their drinking.

Tom swore, of course, and smoked. Smoking did not make a man act foolish and do and say silly things, and it did not cost too much.

His restless spirit could take only a few years at the station, then he was ready for a change. Another year or so he spent roaming up and down between Victoria and northern Queensland, working at many trades and gaining experiences that would stand him in good stead the rest of his life.

When he was 21 Tom found employment at Inverell in northern New South Wales, working for an Englishman named Leslie Mason. The two got along well. In fact, Leslie made no secret of the fact that he had never known such a hard worker. Tom's honesty and capabilities so impressed him that he decided to take a long-anticipated trip back to England and leave his hired hand in sole charge, on a share basis.

But two important events occurred before Leslie and his family left.

The first took place one afternoon when the two men were in the township loading cattle feed. Tom hoisted a full bushel sack onto his shoulder just as Leslie nudged him. "Wait a bit. There's old Mr. Frazer. His mother died last week. I must try and comfort the poor fellow."

Tom nodded. He'd heard of the old bachelor who lived up on the mountain with only his aged mother for company.

The man was about to pass with a simple "Good day," but Mason held out his hand. "I'm sorry to hear about your mother's death, Will. I know you must miss her. But she was a good woman, we all know that. You can rest assured she's up there in heaven with the angels and——"

Frazer shook his hand. "Thank you, Les. I appreciate your kind words. But mother is not in heaven. She's sleeping in her grave until Jesus comes to call her back to life."

Tom's jaw sagged. The two conversed a few minutes longer, but Tom heard nothing more. Frazer's words whirled around in his mind. Not in heaven—sleeping till Jesus comes—— What did the man mean? What sort of heresy was this?

The old man went on his way and Leslie turned back to the loading. Waiting until Will Frazer was out of earshot, Tom exploded, "Did you hear what he said? His mother is not in heaven. She's still in her grave. Why, our minister says——"

"Don't take any notice of Will," his boss soothed. "He's a fine fellow. Honest as the day. But he has some queer ideas about the Bible. He keeps Saturday for the Sabbath day."

"Is he a Jew?"

"No, he's a Seventh-day Adventist."

"Seventh-day Adventist?" Tom had never heard of them. But that long-ago conversation between his mother and Aunt Nell sprang to his mind. "We keep the wrong Sabbath, Nell," his mother had said. "Saturday is the seventh day, not Sunday."

Oh, well, Tom shrugged, at least Mr. Frazer has the day right.

At the moment Tom attended the Church of England. In fact, he was on excellent terms with the Anglican vicar because of his habit of arriving early for 8:00 A.M. Communion. The vicar tried to teach him how to pull the bell ropes that hung inside the steeple.

"Short jerks, Tom. Not long ones. Not so hard, man. Little short jerks like this."

Although Tom never mastered the art of bell ringing, he

basked in the vicar's favor. He enjoyed church, too, though he always squirmed when the congregation repeated the Ten Commandments aloud and then recited, "Lord, have mercy upon us, and incline our hearts to keep this law."

We don't, he thought. At least we don't keep the fourth commandment.

He couldn't get out of his head what his mother's teacher, Mr. Caleb, had said about Saturday being the seventh day. If that was so—and certainly all the calendars that Tom had ever seen put Sunday as the *first* day and Saturday as the *seventh* day—then why were all the Christians going to church on Sunday?

Well, not quite all. Apparently Seventh-day Adventists, whoever they were, observed Saturday for Sunday. But people regarded them as queer, Leslie said. Was it better to be queer and obey God, or——?

"Maybe only the Seventh-day Adventists know about it," Tom mused aloud. "Maybe everyone else thinks that *Sunday* is the *seventh* day."

Even as he said it, he realized that he was wrong. Leslie knew, and Tom's mother—years and years ago—and anyone who gave it any thought would recognize that Sunday was *not* the seventh day. "Then none of us are obeying the commandments properly," he decided. With a shrug he rolled himself another cigarette.

Still he attended the Anglican services. Leslie and his family were also Anglicans, but sometimes they went to the Methodist church with their friends, or to the Presbyterian church. Tom went along with them, but the services failed to satisfy him. Restless and disillusioned, his church attendance soon became sporadic. Finally he gave up going at all.

The other far-reaching event that took place before Leslie left for England was Rosie's arrival.

Rosie Lewin was Mrs. Mason's sister. With the excitement and preparations for a journey to far-off England looming ahead, Mrs. Mason sent for her to come from Sydney and help her sew clothes for the trip.

Tom was only mildly curious when Leslie brought his sister-in-law home. At suppertime his employer introduced them to each other, and he said, "How d'ya do?" in the approved manner, noting that Rosie had blue eyes like her sister, and that was that.

But as the days passed, the sight of her fair head bent over her sewing and her slim, white fingers busily plying the shining needle did strange things to his breathing. Tom thought he had never seen such a pretty girl, nor heard such a gentle voice, or known such friendliness. Rosie exuded lovingkindness as a rose did perfume.

But she did not respond to him as quickly. From her brother-in-law he learned that she had recently broken her engagement to a young city man, who was now threatening to sue her for breach of promise. "I don't really think he'll take her to court," Leslie said. "But it has her a bit upset. Shows what kind of fellow he is, doesn't it?"

"Indeed it does," Tom said, clenching his fists. He'd like to teach that city slicker a thing or two.

For a while Tom acted toward Rosie with the respectful reticence due a beautiful girl with a broken heart. But gradually he took courage as her smiles and shy glances conveyed the message that her heart was not all that badly broken.

Their courtship, begun smoothly enough, soon ran into bumps and jolts because of their differences in background. Used to earning her own living as a seamstress, Rosie moved and spoke with the sophisticated ease of a city girl accustomed to mixing with white-collar people. His slipshod country speech vexed her. "Don't say, 'Didya? Wotchawant?'," she chided gently when they were alone. "Say, 'Did you? What do you want? Please, may I?'"

His manners were not up to her standards either. When they chanced to meet another lady, he touched his hat and bowed slightly. But that was not sufficient for her. "You should take your hat *right off* when you bow," she insisted. "That's not being sissy. That's etiquette."

Etiquette or not, he had had enough. Plenty of other girls

would love him the way he was, and not want to change him—"trying to make a silk purse out of a sow's ear," as Abe Crabtree used to say.

Without a word one night he left her at her sister's door, leaped onto his horse, and galloped a couple of times around the paddock before heading for the house gate. But Rosie reached it before him.

"Tom," she panted, "I didn't mean it. It's *you* I love, not your manners."

All the same it took two years for her ambitious family to become reconciled to her engagement to a "country bumpkin." They never quite forgave him for capturing her heart.

By the time the Masons returned from England, Tom's portion of the share-farming venture netted him £300, a goodly sum back in 1923. With his earnings, plus Rosie's savings from her seamstress business, they purchased a little farm near Inverell and set up housekeeping.

But bad luck dogged them from the start. The end of their second year of marriage found her with a 6-month-old son and a dying husband.

For days Tom had ignored the pain in his side. "It's nothing," he told his wife. "Maybe I've strained a muscle or something. No, I'm too busy to go to a doctor. What do those quacks know, anyhow?"

By the time his agony drove him to seek help, it was too late. The doctor operated, but Tom's appendix had ruptured and spread its poison through his body. Peritonitis set in, and abscesses began forming on his bowel.

"I'm afraid your husband is in a bad way." The doctor looked pityingly at young Mrs. Crabtree and her baby. "Can you stay in town to be near him?"

"No." She shook her head. "I must go back to the farm. There are cows to milk, chickens to feed . . ."

The physician understood. "Come back tomorrow, and we'll let you see him." He patted her arm in fatherly fashion. "Rest assured that we'll do everything we can."

The next day Rosie harnessed old Bess to the sulky and drove into the hospital to visit Tom. A rosy-cheeked nurse took her into the ward. "He's very ill. Don't stay too long," she admonished in a throaty whisper.

With a rustle of starched apron the nurse swept out, and Rosie stared aghast at the man in the high, white bed. Was this pallid-faced stranger her husband? Her Tommy? How could he have changed in so short a time? She sank onto a hard chair beside the bed and took his hand in hers. He opened his eyes briefly. "Hello, dear. How's the baby?"

Hours passed. Her husband scarcely stirred or spoke. It came time to leave and she stood up. She leaned over and kissed Tom. "I'll come again tomorrow," she whispered and tried to stifle the catch in her voice. Would he still be here tomorrow?

Mechanically Rosie untied the horse and headed back along the road to the farm. Tears blinded her eyes, and occasionally she sobbed aloud. Tom was dying. No one had to tell her that. The sulky wheels slowed and she flipped the leather reins automatically. Quiet old Bess's steady plodding quickened a fraction. Her tears splashed onto the baby sleeping on her lap. Whom could she turn to? What could she do?

"Oh, God, make him better," she pleaded aloud. Suddenly her thoughts flew back across the years to the book that her mother had bought. One morning, long ago, a young man came to the door selling a book called *Heralds of the Morning.* The Lewin household had ample money, and her mother bought it. But she did not read it. In fact no one in the family had except little Rosie.

Heralds of the Morning fascinated her. The pictures of Jesus coming with a cloud of angels made her shiver with mingled delight and dread. Curled up in a comfortable chair, she read the book from cover to cover. A lot of it she did not understand, but it convinced her that Jesus was returning soon and filled her with secret fears that He might appear before she was ready.

Now Rosie remembered. With sudden decision she pulled the reins tightly. "Whoa! Bess. Whoa!" With a surprised snort the horse obediently stood still between the sulky shafts. Holding her baby in her arms, Rosie climbed down and walked a short distance from the road. Then she kneeled behind a bush.

"Dear God." Her tears streamed afresh. "God, I read Your book. I know Jesus is coming back soon. God, I'll serve You for the rest of my life if only You will heal my husband."

For some minutes she remained on her knees, quietly sobbing out her pleas and promises. Presently a sense of peace stole over her. She knew God had accepted her promises and that He would heal Tom.

With a light heart Rosie scrambled to her feet. "Daddy is going to get well," she told her infant. She kissed him, clambered awkwardly up into the sulky, and headed back to the hospital.

In the meantime Tom's doctor came in to see him. "Are you a Christian, Mr. Crabtree?" he asked soberly.

"Yes," Tom groaned through his pain. His head throbbed, his body burned, and he never felt less like thinking about religion. He didn't attend church anymore, and he wasn't sure what the doctor was getting at, but at least he wasn't a heathen, so he must be a Christian.

"Then, Mr. Crabtree, you'd better pray to God to heal you. There's nothing more that I can do."

A strained silence fell between them. Then Tom opened pain-filled eyes. "You could give me a drink of water."

"Oh, no, Mr. Crabtree," the alarmed physician protested. "If you drank anything, it would kill you. You'd start to vomit and that would be the end of you."

The hot November sun blazed on the hospital's iron roof, and the air in the ward was oven-hot. Thirty hours had passed since Tom had tasted food or drink, and the longing for a cup of cold water nearly drove him crazy. "I'll die right now if you don't give me a drink." His parched lips cracked as he formed the words. Let it kill him. He might as well go one way as another.

The doctor hesitated. Then he shrugged and went outside. In a few moments he returned with a glass of water. Tom downed it at a gulp. The doctor took the glass and hurriedly left the ward, his ethics shattered.

Presently a young probationer nurse pattered in. "Is there anything I can do for you, Mr. Crabtree?" she asked.

"Yes," he nodded. "The doctor's just been here. He said I can have water now. Will you get me a glass?"

The nurse brought him one, and Tom drained it eagerly. Then he sank back on his pillows and smiled. He felt the water going right through his body—cleansing, cooling. Now, he knew he would recover.

At that moment Rosie walked into the ward, her face bright with hope. One glance at Tom and she knew the miracle had already happened. "Darling, you look so much better."

"Yes." His voice was strong. "I'll be out of here in no time."

But he wasn't. Six weeks passed before the doctor allowed him to put even a toe out of bed, and much longer than that before he could go home.

Those long weeks of inactivity gave Tom plenty of time to think. Rosie told him about her prayer and her promise to God, and he agreed with her that as soon as he was well enough they must begin attending church regularly. But even as he said it, the old rebellion welled up inside him. What's the use? he thought. None of the churches *really* obey God's commandments.

Then one day Tom discovered that Mrs. Bartlett, a patient in the next ward, was a Seventh-day Adventist. Nearly every day someone brought 3-year-old Norma Bartlett to visit her mother, and while the adults talked, the little girl explored her strange surroundings. She often wandered into Tom's room, and by the time he was well enough to sit in the sunshine on the hospital veranda, they had become friends.

Soon after that Mrs. Bartlett transferred to a daybed on the veranda, and the circle of friendship expanded to include her, Mr. Bartlett, and Rosie.

During one of their long conversations Mrs. Bartlett mentioned that she was a Seventh-day Adventist. She did not parade her religion, but her kind manner and her evident joy impressed Tom.

She's a Seventh-day Adventist, and she's not queer, he reflected, and all those Seventh-day Adventists who visit her seem to be nice people and quite normal. Perhaps Leslie meant that only their religion is strange.

During his time in hospital Tom's friends and neighbors rallied round to harvest his grain crop and do what they could to help Rosie keep the farm going. Even after he went home they lent him a hand. It took a long time for his strength to return, and the weeks stretched into months before he felt able to take on his full load.

Some months after he returned to work he came in for his midday meal, and his wife showed him a paper.

"See this, Tom. It's called *The Youth's Instructor.* A Church of Christ minister called at the house this morning and gave it to me. He says he'll return tonight to give us a Bible study."

Tom gave the paper a cursory glance. "I don't want any Church of Christ minister in my house," he growled.

Her face fell. Daily she remembered the promise she had made to God: "I'll follow you always if you will spare my husband's life." Suddenly she brightened. "Oh, Tom, I made a mistake. It wasn't the Church of Christ. He said he was a Seventh-day Adventist minister."

"Then that's all right," her husband grunted. "I don't mind if he stops by, then. I'll invite our neighbors across to hear him too. They're always ribbing me about the Sunday-night meetings that the Seventh-day Adventists are having in the Town Hall. They reckon I ought to go along, because the Seventh-day Adventist ministers would convert me for sure."

That night Pastor C. J. Reynolds came to the house armed with his Bible and another book that had pictures of all kinds of weird animals and things that he called prophetic symbols. Tom never forgot his presentation of the prophecy of the second chapter of Daniel. As he went about his farm work the next day, the golden-headed image haunted him, and the words "They shall not cleave one to another."

Tom remembered the Great War. Charlie and David had fought in it. The German Kaiser had wanted to unite Europe then, and where had it got him? Nowhere. Just like Charlemagne, Napoleon, and the others. "They shall not cleave one to another," God said.

For two years the Bible studies continued, and Tom stubbornly resisted the Spirit of God. Some nights, after the pastor left, Tom rolled sleeplessly on his bed, tortured by mental agony. "They're right. Everything they teach is from the Bible," he'd say to Rosie. "Someday I'll have to become a Seventh-day Adventist. I know it. Someday—but I can't now. We've got to get this farm established first."

Tom took to drinking to ease the torment of his accusing conscience. Then Rosie trembled, and Lindsay and Baby Barry cried in fear when they heard their father's faltering footsteps on the creaking veranda boards.

His wife did her best to keep her promise to God. She read her Bible, prayed often, and tried to rear her little boys to love Jesus. Neither Pastor Reynolds nor any of the other Seventh-day Adventists dared come near the place. The Bible studies had ended with Tom shouting, "Get off my property, you Adventists! Leave me and my family alone."

Months passed. Then one rainy day when the wet ground was too muddy for plowing, Tom took his gun down from the shed wall and stamped into the kitchen. "I'm going to shoot some of those pesky rabbits," he growled. "They eat the best of every so-and-so crop I try to raise."

Rosie said nothing. In fact, she rarely spoke much anymore. It wasn't safe. His temper flared at the slightest provocation.

Tom saddled his horse and rode into the township to purchase a box of cartridges. His route led past the little Seventh-day Adventist church, and when he saw the people assembling there, he remembered that it was Saturday, God's Sabbath day.

"Oh, curse them!" he muttered. Pulling his hat well down over his face, he spurred his horse to a gallop, but he was too late. Some of the church members standing outside waved, and he knew that they had recognized him. Now they'd go in and tell everyone, and the congregation would start praying for him. He swore under his breath. Would he never be rid of those Adventists?

When he reached home again, Tom rode down to the farthest paddock and loaded his gun. "Whoa, girl, whoa." He reined his horse. They'd only need to remain still a few minutes and the rabbits would pop out of their burrows. The animals liked dull, cool days. "Ah!" His sharp eyes caught a movement, and he raised his gun to his shoulder.

Tom's first shot startled his normally quiet horse. It reared and bolted madly across the paddock, flinging him off into a jumble of jagged rocks piled in one corner of the fence.

When Tom regained consciousness the blood on his shirt had dried, and the westering sun told him that he had lain among the rocks for more than five hours. Dizzily he sat up and looked around. His horse grazed quietly at the far end of the long paddock. He had no hope of catching it. Lurching toward the fence, he clutched at the rails. If he could hold onto the fence he'd be all right. Weakly he staggered from post to post until he was close enough to home for Rosie to hear his calls for help.

Startled, she raced from the house with the little boys at her heels. "Oh, Tom, you're hurt." Her voice trembled as she took his arm and guided him toward the veranda. "What happened?"

"The horse bolted." Her husband groaned and crawled painfully up the steep back steps. "Threw me onto the rocks."

Somehow he completed the climb and collapsed in a heap at the top of the steps. She and the boys had a hard time pushing and dragging him into the bedroom. "Tom, you're too heavy. I can't lift you." Her voice sounded desperate. "If we all help, can you heave yourself up onto the bed?"

They could not understand his reply, but finally their

combined efforts got him into bed, and Rosie fetched towels and warm water and bathed away the blood. The fall had cut and bruised his back and shoulders, but the ugly gash in the back of his head was the worst.

"You'll have to go to the doctor, Tom." Frightened tears welled in her troubled eyes. "I'm sure your head will have to be stitched. I can see your skull. I'll ask Mr. Lyall to take you into town."

With only a hurricane lantern to guide her, Rosie stumbled out into the night. Through knee-deep mud she somehow found her way through the fences and across paddocks to the neighbors' house.

The Lyalls had recently purchased a new Chevrolet car. Without hesitating a moment they put Mrs. Crabtree into it and both of them accompanied her back home—Mrs. Lyall to stay with the little boys and her husband to help Rosie get Tom into the back seat.

She sat beside her husband, pillowing his head against the bumps and jolts. Tom groaned and cried out in agony at every movement. He felt sure he would not survive the drive.

The doctor stitched Tom's scalp and put him in the hospital again. All night a nurse sat by him, and early in the morning the doctor came to his bedside. "Well, you're still alive. I was afraid the shock would kill you. You can go home, Mr. Crabtree, if you promise to stay in bed for a month. Your brain is all shaken up. Concussion is dangerous, and you must have rest and quiet."

Some of the Seventh-day Adventists heard about Tom's accident and visted him. "If you had been in church with us that Sabbath," they said, "this would not have happened." One after another, his Adventist callers repeated their warning. His anger mounted. Pastor Reynolds' visit was the final straw.

"I'm sorry to hear about your accident," he said. "But 'whom the Lord loveth he chasteneth,' you know, 'and scourgeth every son whom he receiveth.'" He meant it to be comforting, but Tom's seething temper exploded.

"The Lord hasn't received me," he retorted. "You go on

home and forget about me. You Adventists are a blasted lot of Job's comforters, that's what you are. Go on home, Pastor, and don't come back."

Reynolds did not return, nor did any of the other Adventists. Three lonely weeks passed; then one morning Rosie reported that the cows had broken into the wheat field.

He swore under his breath. It was something that Rosie could not handle. Concussion or not, he had to save his cows—and his wheat. Ignoring her protests, he struggled weakly into his clothes and tottered down to the field. With the help of the dogs he chased the cows out and then repaired the fence. But when he tried to herd a particularly obstinate cow into the home yard, she lashed out and caught him a hard kick on his ankle.

Tom fell to the ground, moaning and swearing in helpless agony. He was too far away from the house for his wife to hear him call; yet he could not walk. For a few minutes he lay there wondering what to do. Then he raised his head and saw an old broomstick propped against the fence in a corner of the yard. It took half an hour of excruciating endeavor, but eventually he reached the stick, and, using it as a crutch, he hopped and hobbled up to the house and collapsed onto the nearest chair.

His groans brought Rosie running. "What have you done now?"

Once again she helped him into bed. Whatever she might have thought, she said nothing. Instead she hurried back and forth, carrying cold water and thick towels to pack the swollen, black leg in cold compresses. For more than an hour she worked over him, changing the towels, soaking them, wringing them out, and placing them carefully on his injured leg.

"I'll have to go and prepare dinner now, Tom. Does it feel any better?"

"A little."

She went out to the kitchen, and he heard her stoking up the fire and clattering the saucepans. The little boys played in the back yard. He could not mistake the "squeak, creek" as their rope swing on the old gum tree swayed back and forth.

Left alone, he began to take stock of himself. It is more than a coincidence, he mused. God must be allowing all his suffering to bring him to a realization of what he must do. For long minutes his thoughts flew back over the events of the past few months, the past few years. Was it all chance, or was there some design in everything that had happened? He must know.

Painfully he slid out of bed and onto his knees. "Is this what it's all about, Lord? Are You trying to teach me something?"

The more he thought about it, the more convicted he became. Finally he said, "Lord, today is Sunday. If my ankle is better tomorrow so that I can walk and work, I promise you that I will keep the next Sabbath day holy."

As he said those words a great peace settled over him. For a moment longer he knelt humbly before the Lord. Then he crawled back into bed and fell asleep.

Early the next morning Tom got out of bed. His ankle still looked black, but he felt no pain. Gingerly he put on his boots and walked across the bedroom floor and out into the hall. God had answered his prayer. He could walk. After breakfast he yoked up the horses and went off to plow his fields.

Tom plowed all morning and experienced no pain. Not the slightest twinge. The Lord had certainly fulfilled His part of the bargain.

During the afternoon he heard voices. Shading his eyes with his hand, he saw two men coming across the field toward him. One of them looked like Pastor Reynolds. Yes, it was, and he had another man with him. Funny that he should come today. Was it significant?

The three men talked for about half an hour. They discussed crops and cattle and weather conditions. The stranger was a visiting pastor from Sydney. He said he'd like to see Tom again, and Crabtree promised that he would attend the evangelistic meetings held in the Town Hall each Sunday night.

"Right you are, Tom. We'll see you there." After they shook hands all round, the pastors went up to the house to visit with Rosie and the boys. Tom started the horses on another round of the field, but a voice seemed to say to him, "I thought you promised that you'd attend church on Sabbath, not the mission meeting on Sunday night."

Well, yes, I did, he admitted. I said if my ankle was better.

"It was better, wasn't it?"

Yes. But it was still black and swollen. Maybe the absence of pain was only coincidence. Perhaps it would have gotten better anyway, without any prayers and promises.

So the battle with the Voice raged back and forth in Tom's heart, until suddenly, loud and clear, he heard the words *"This is the last time."*

That settled it. Tom unhitched the team and took the horses to the feed paddock. Then he went home.

Rosie met him at the door. "The pastor came to visit," she beamed. "He's agreed to come and study the Bible with us again." Her eyes searched his face for his reaction, but he said nothing.

After they ate supper, Tom wandered restlessly around the house for a while, and then they went to bed. Rosie fell asleep as soon as her head hit the pillow, but her husband tossed and turned for hours, weighing everything in his mind. After all, what was stopping him from becoming a Seventh-day Adventist? He believed everything they taught. All their doctrines were Bible based. Why was he delaying? Finally he faced the fact. Pride, willful stubborn pride, was all that held him back. Fear of what the neighbors would say when they found out that Tom—hard drinking, hard swearing, fierce-tempered Tom—had "got religion."

Thursday night came, and Pastor Reynolds arrived as promised. The three of them sat around the kitchen table, and the minister opened his Bible. He took as his subject the unpardonable sin. Tom's heart throbbed to every word of it, and when the pastor ended with the text " 'What shall it profit a man, if he shall gain the whole world, and lose his own soul?' " he had a hard time keeping his composure.

Reverently the pastor closed his Bible and turned to Rosie. "Well, dear girl, what about it?"

"Ask Tom." Her nervous fingers plucked at the edge of the tablecloth.

Pastor Reynolds turned to him. "You bound me never to ask you to become a Seventh-day Adventist, Tom, and I've kept my word. But what about it? Will you give your heart to the Lord tonight?"

"Yes," he replied quickly. "I have decided to do just that."

For a moment there was an incredulous silence. Then tears rolled down the minister's cheeks. He grasped Tom's hand and said brokenly, "Praise God for that."

Rosie burst into uncontrollable weeping and crumpled with the shock. It was many weeks before her nerves returned to normal.

"But will you let me smoke?" Tom's nicotine-stained hand reached into his pocket.

"It's not for me to tell you what to do. You have given your heart to God, Tom. You ask the Holy Spirit to guide you."

"Then take it all." Tom's hand came out of his pocket, and he thrust his pipe and tobacco pouch toward the pastor. "Take it, and pray to the Lord to give me victory over the habit."

The Lord answered those prayers. Never again did Tom feel the slightest craving for either tobacco or alcohol.

The next day was Friday. Preparation day, the Seventh-day Adventists called it. Tom knew what it meant. Everything had to be ready for the Sabbath. Just as long ago on Saturdays he had blacked the boots and carried in extra firewood for Sunday, so now he must do all the extra chores on Friday.

I'll hurry through my work and get back to the house before sunset, he planned to himself. Then I can have my bath and be all ready for Sabbath.

On the first round of the field the plow hit a stump, and the main bar, to which all eight horses were harnessed, broke in two. Worse than that, the horses scattered, sending hooks and nuts and bolts flying all over the furrows, and taking much of the harness and parts of the plow with them.

Without wasting a moment in self-pity, Tom started after them on foot. Calling and coaxing, he eventually rounded up all the horses and tied them to the fence. Then he searched up and down the nearer furrows and over the yet unplowed ground. As he searched, he prayed. When he had the last nut and bolt safely in his pockets, he thanked God and started back to the workshop. The next item was to fashion another twelve-foot-long main bar and fasten everything together again.

Tom squinted at the sun. By the time he finished all that, he would have no time left for plowing. With a resigned shrug he went down to the field and untied the horses. When he had them safely in their feeding paddock, he secured the gate and set off for the house. Only then did he think of something.

The marvel of it made him pull up with a jerk. He stood stock-still in the middle of the yard and his jaw sagged—he had not sworn all day! Through all that trouble with the horses, despite all the turmoil of broken bars and lost bolts and hooks, not a single oath had escaped his lips.

"What hath God wrought!" Reverently Tom bowed his head. It seemed only yesterday that one of his neighbors had ridden over to him in the paddock and asked him to be more careful with his language. "Our house is nearly a mile away, Tom, but my wife can hear you swearing at your horses."

And now, without his being aware of it, God had taken away the swearing, along with the desire to smoke and drink.

Four months after their baptism, a crisis arose when Pastor Reynolds examined the subject of tithing with them. Of course, he had mentioned it during previous Bible studies, but Tom had brushed it aside along with anything else that he found distasteful. Now he must face the matter head on.

"What shall we do?" he asked his wife after the minister left. "A tenth of our income seems a lot of money when we have so little. We never have a penny to spare as it is."

She did not reply. Long ago she had made her full commitment to God. Her husband must make his own decision.

Tom picked up a pencil and scrawled figures in the margin of an old newspaper. He added and subtracted and scratched his head and chewed the end of the pencil. Eventually he looked up. "We've been in the church for four months. In that time we've earned about £170. That means £17 tithe. I don't see how we can do it. Not a grain of that winter wheat I sowed came up. I need to buy chaff to feed the horses."

"How much will a ton of it cost?"

"Seventeen pounds."

Silence fell between them. He tapped the table with his pencil. Rosie nervously smoothed the folds of her skirt with work-worn fingers. The battered old alarm clock on the mantle shelf ticked loudly. Presently he spoke.

"Y'know, Rosie, I think we should pay the tithe and ask God to send us rain." Pushing his chair back, he reached for the checkbook behind the clock.

"So do I." Her relieved smile radiated confidence.

Tom wrote out the check for £17 tithe, and they knelt together beside the old wooden kitchen table, asking God to supply their needs according to His promises in Malachi 3:8-12.

That same week the rain came—days of steady downpour that soaked the parched earth. Tom's spring-planted maize sprang to life and pushed up slender green spikes. Long after the rain stopped, the ground was too soggy for him to cultivate between the rows, and weeds and thistles flourished unchecked. But that maize grew and grew. Never in all his life had he seen such a crop. Not only did it provide plenty of feed for the horses but he sold the surplus for £400 and bought twenty cows.

THOMAS CRABTREE,
GOD'S MAN

All might have gone well if Tom had been content to build up his herd and become a dairy farmer. Even during world depression dairying provided at least a meager living. But Tom came from the wide, wheat-growing plains of Victoria, and the grain was in his blood.

Stubbornly he struggled on against drought, disease, and prices as low as fifteen pence a bushel for wheat in 1929 and 1930, and £2 a ton for chaff. Lack of rain was the biggest problem. Week after dragging week the searing sun blazed from a brassy sky. Crops shriveled and trees drooped as plants and animals suffered alike.

The dam dried up, and Tom had to drive the cows a mile across the fields to drink at a muddy stream. It was hard on both man and beast, and it took time from his other work—too much time. "Could we sink a well?" Rosie asked one day.

"I've thought of that. It would cost a lot of money, and then there's no certainty that we would find water."

"Perhaps we should try."

Putting on his best clothes, Tom went to see the bank manager, that harassed individual already "carrying" more than half the farmers in the district. Tom's persuasive arguments won the day. Assessors visited the farm, the bank drew up mortgage papers, and the well drillers moved onto the property.

Days of anxiety followed as the bore bit deep into the sun-baked earth, through soil and sand, rock and shale, ever downward. Three hundred feet. Four hundred feet. Five hundred feet. Tom nearly tore his hair out, and the drill operators looked more grim with each passing hour.

"I dunno whether we orta——" the well boss scratched his head. And then, just at the crucial moment, the shout arose, "Water! Water!"

At five hundred and five feet they struck water. But the £1,000 it cost to sink the bore crippled Tom's chances of success.

In vain he tried to sell the property. No one had money to buy. Everyone was in the same financial boat. In the cities, dole lines of hopeless men wound snakelike around the blocks of shops and offices. In the country the farmers hung on, glad to grow enough food to feed their own families.

For a long time Tom and Rosie struggled on. They were never hungry, but they had no money to repay their loans. Eventually the bank foreclosed the mortgage and they had to walk off the farm with nothing to show for their eight years of hard work.

Now he and his wife and their four children became nomads. Back and forth across New South Wales and Victoria they wandered. Finding six months' work here, three months' there. Drought and depression held the country in its iron grip, but the young Crabtrees were no worse off than anyone else, and better off than some. At least they always had full stomachs, clothes on their backs, and a roof of some sort over their heads.

In the course of time their travels led them to the far north coast of New South Wales. There hardy pioneers had moved in and cleared the untouched land, ready to plant banana suckers in the rich red soil.

Tom picked up a handful of earth and let it run through his fingers. His heart leaped with hope. If only he could have some of the land. Then he could carve out a place for himself and his family.

But it was no time for dreaming the impossible. He had Rosie and the four children to support. Dear Rosie. Never once did she reproach him for their misfortunes, or for being a bad manager and losing all of her money, as well as his own. But her family did. They were loud and bitter in their accusations, and Tom was glad to put as many miles as possible between himself and them.

For several days he tramped around the plantations in Burringbar asking for work. No one could afford to hire any help, but they were all friendly, and Tom kept his eyes and ears open and acquired a great deal of information about banana growing. The more he learned, the more enthusiastic he became. If—if only——

Eventually he found a job. Not with bananas, but back to the blistering, backbreaking labor of felling trees and clearing the prickly-leafed lantana off the land so someone else could plant and grow. "Two pounds a week, Tom, and you and your family can live in the farmhouse until the job is finished," Mr. Bullman said.

Even the prospect of digging five acres of root-matted, steeply-sloping hillside with a mattock failed to daunt him. He was so thankful to have some income and somewhere to live that he fled into the bush and wept.

When that grueling contract finished, Tom took his family to the nearby Brunswick Heads for a short holiday. He had never seen the sea until that Christmas of 1932, and he was as excited as his youngest child at the sight of that vast expanse of white-capped blue water.

Brunswick Heads was a favorite holiday resort, and Seventh-day Adventists from miles around were among those who pitched their tents along the narrow riverbank. On Sabbath they all congregated under the trees and held their Sabbath school and church service. The Chilcotts and Parmenters came from Burringbar, and the Locks, Scarrs, and Arthurs from Lismore. Pastor Reynolds vacationed there, and the Wyborns and other Sabbathkeepers journeyed from the surrounding districts.

"It's just like heaven!" Rosie whispered, and her husband nodded. After months of isolation it was indeed wonderful to be able to study the Bible and talk with fellow believers. The friendships formed that Yule season lasted until death.

With the brief holiday over, Tom hurried back to work. Next

he helped build a road around the mountain so that Mr. Mikks could transport the bananas from his proposed plantation. All the while he dug and chipped and smoothed and lugged rocks out of the way, his admiration for the soil grew. If only he could afford to buy a few acres of it, his fortune would be made.

Suddenly an idea struck him with such force that he ceased digging and leaned on his pick handle to think the thing through. Certainly he could not buy, since he could not borrow money without security. But, could he rent? Was there any way he could lease some of the fertile soil?

Tom was not the kind of man to let a good idea go unnourished. That afternoon he mentioned the matter to Mr. Mikks. "You can get that idea out of your head," his employer laughed. "I've leased the whole lot from Mr. Steer, and I'm going to plant it all next year."

Something about the hollowness of his laugh told Tom that he was lying. He said nothing, but old Abe's cunning, which he had inherited, welled up inside him. As soon as he got home from work, he put on a clean shirt and trousers and walked across the hill to call on Mr. Steer.

"Good evening, Mr. Steer," he said when the sedate English bachelor opened the door. "My name is Tom Crabtree. I have come all the way from Victoria in the hope of growing bananas. Burringbar is a fine place, and I would like to rent some of the land that you have here. But Mr. Mikks says that you have promised it all to him."

"Indeed, I have done nothing of the sort!" The man's well-bred English composure scarcely veiled his indignation. "If you have the money to pay, you're as welcome to lease it as anyone else is."

Tom took a deep breath. With a prayer in his heart he looked Percy Steer straight in the eye. "I have no money at all, sir. But I have a wife and four children to support, and, God helping me, I can work as hard as two men."

A shadow crossed the landowner's kind face. "But how will you live in the meantime? It requires eighteen months for banana plants to grow—two years before you'd make any money out of them."

"I know. I'll have to keep on taking any kind of occasional work that I can get to keep me going."

"H'mm. Yes, I suppose you stand a better chance of casual work if you are on the spot." He leaned across the table and picked up a pencil and paper. After a bit of figuring he said, "Now, look, I'll let you rent ten acres at £3 per acre per annum. How's that?"

Tom nodded slowly. If only he had some money. The current market price for land was only £6 per acre. But, he shrugged mentally, £3 was the regular rent paid on banana country. The man asked nothing more than his due. Aloud he said, "Thank you, Mr. Steer."

But Percy Steer seemed unhappy. Stirring uneasily in his chair, he tapped a five-finger exercise on his trousered knee. Presently he burst out, "I tell you what, Tom. It's going to be two years before you earn a penny out of bananas. I'll let you have two years rent free if you do some clearing and fencing for me."

"Righto!" Crabtree's face lighted up like a gas lamp.

But Mr. Steer had thought of another problem. "Where will you live?"

"We're in Mr. Bullman's house now. But if you will let me have the trees I fell as I clear the land, I'll split them and build a slab house."

"Of course, of course. Take all the timber you want. There's an old banana shed at the back of my place. You can have the roofing iron off that, if you like, and any of the posts that are sound."

"Thank you, sir." Tom beamed. God was good to him.

He set to work with a will. Whenever he could, he took on day labor for others in order to earn money for food and other necessities. But evenings and Sundays he toiled for himself: chopping down trees, brushing out weeds and lantana, hoeing and digging, carving a plantation out of the bush.

Rosie and the children helped too. It was a family affair, just as it had been in Tom's youth when he and his brothers had worked with their mother to clear land for their wheat farm.

More than a year passed before a house with rough timber posts and walls rose on a cleared space on top of the hill. A roving hobo-carpenter, glad to work for his food and a small daily wage, helped Tom with the doors and window frames. Rosie tacked tightly stretched hessian* between the studs and divided the interior of the house into four rooms. Then little daughter Norma helped her to mix buckets of flour paste and to paper the hessian walls with glossy colored pictures cut from the Sunday *Mail*.

Scrounging around on the town's rubbish dump, Tom found an old wood-burning cookstove, and triumphantly bore it home. The bottom had rusted out and the door hung rakishly on corroded hinges. But he wired the broken pieces together and mixed sand, lime, and clay to cement the old stove into place. For eight years Rosie baked bread and cakes and did all the family cooking with it.

What furniture they could not fashion from ingenuity, empty crates, and cretonne, they reluctantly purchased at the secondhand market. The Crabtrees were poor, yes, but it did not worry them. Thousands of others were even worse off.

One sunny Sunday, Tom and his sons were hard at work felling trees and splitting them to make fence posts, when Percy Steer came across from his plantation. A worried frown marred his usually genial face, and he came straight to the point.

"Tom," he said, "I don't want you and the boys to work on Sundays. I'm a Sabbathkeeper, and the Ten Commandments say that we should keep the Sabbath holy. It says, 'the stranger within thy gates' too, and that means you, Tom, when you're working on my land."

"All right, Mr. Steer." Tom touched his hat respectfully. "If you don't want me to work on Sundays, I won't. There's plenty I can do around my own house. But, Mr. Steer, I've kept the Sabbath already."

"What do you mean?" The Englishman looked startled. "This is Sunday. There is only one Sabbath."

---

* A coarse sacking of hemp or hemp and jute.

"Mr. Steer, when you go back to your house, look on your calendar and you will see that Sunday is the *first* day of the week. I keep Saturday, the *seventh* day, just as the fourth commandment says we should."

"Wha—what are you?" Mr. Steer's voice betrayed his bewilderment.

"I'm a Seventh-day Adventist."

"Never heard of them." For a few seconds Mr. Steer lapsed into silence. Considering the interview closed, Tom started to walk away, when his employer spoke. "This is a new thought to me, Tom. Will you come down to my house sometime and we'll talk about it?"

"Of course. I'll be glad to."

Not too many nights elapsed before Tom arrived with his Bible on Mr. Steer's doorstep, and the two men studied far into the night. The next week they met again and discussed another Bible topic. A knowledgable Bible student, Percy Steer within a few months accepted the seventh-day Sabbath, the second coming of Christ, and the other Bible doctrines that Tom pointed out to him. Soon Jim Musk, another neighbor, joined them, and those two were Tom's first converts in the Burringbar district.

Back in 1933 Seventh-day Adventist country churches were not numerous, but the local conferences had a concern for their isolated members. As often as possible during the year, ministers and conference staff members visited them, and between times the mail brought a steady supply of tracts and the *Signs* magazine.

One time the visiting minister urged Tom to Ingather in the Burringbar district. "This territory has never been done before, Tom, and we need all the funds we can gather for our island missions."

Harvest Ingathering was something new to Tom, but he tackled it as heartily as he did everything else. Every call at a home became an evangelistic visit. He not only collected a sizable sum for the mission project but gathered enough interests to begin a series of meetings in the house of a friendly

Christian family.

After they finished their long day's work, as many as twenty-five men and women—mostly men, since the women had to stay at home and care for their children—gathered to study God's Word. Some of the young fellows brought their harmonicas with them. One man had an old accordion and another a violin. The woman of the house played on her tinny piano, and everyone sang the hymns. The mountains reverberated with the volume of the sound.

Occasionally the nearest Seventh-day Adventist minister met with them, but mostly Tom and Mr. Chilcott, from a neighboring valley conducted the meetings.

Tom trod the rugged hills barefoot with only a hurricane lantern to light his way. His one pair of boots, old and resoled, he kept in treasured reserve for Sabbaths and special occasions. On his night walks Tom tied the laces together and slung the precious boots over his shoulder. At the foot of the hill below the hostess' house, he waded into the creek and washed the mud off before pushing his wet feet into the boots and tramping up to the door.

Seven people were baptized as a result of the meetings, and many more felt convicted but put off their decision until later. Some delayed too long, and their love for God's truth turned to hate. They ridiculed and hindered Adventists in every possible way.

Every Sabbath the new believers met in Percy Steer's house. The women sat on chairs if there were enough to go around. The men balanced gingerly on thin wooden banana cases, and the children hunkered on the floor. Percy got out his fiddle and everyone joined in singing. Then they studied the Bible lessons together—the adults in Percy's living room and the children shepherded out to the kitchen with one of the women to tell them Bible stories and review their memory verses. They had no finger plays, flannelgraphs, blackboards, sand trays, or offering devices. But that little bush Sabbath school produced some of Australia's finest Adventist leaders.

Later on Percy Steer donated a fine piece of land near

Burringbar township, and the Adventist members scrimped and saved and sacrificed until they raised £35, sufficient to purchase the old weatherboard church, pulpit, and pews from the Corndale Adventists. Willing hands knocked the building to pieces, loaded it onto a borrowed truck, and joyfully transported it to Burringbar, where it was rebuilt.

Three weeks later a cyclone hit the little town and blew down the church. A cry of glee rippled through the community. "The Grass-eaters' church is down! The Grass-eaters' church is down! They'll never get it up again."

But they did. With Tom and Mr. Chilcott as the driving force, the church members rallied to the scene, cut new posts, and reerected the church, stronger and better than ever.

The Week of Prayer of 1935 found Tom at an all-time low financially. Ever since they had become Seventh-day Adventists he and Rosie had managed to put ten shillings—a week's wages—into the annual Week of Sacrifice Offering. But this year ten shillings was all the money he had in the world, with no prospect of getting more.

"We're out of flour," Rosie said on Friday night. "I could only bake enough bread for Sabbath, Tom. There'll be nothing left for Sunday's breakfast. Do you think the offering could wait awhile?"

"No." He shook his head stubbornly. "We've always put at least ten shillings in the Week of Prayer offering, and we'll do the same this year. The Lord will provide. He always has."

His wife nodded. If she worried about what to give her hungry brood for breakfast on Sunday morning, she gave no sign.

The family enjoyed Sabbath with the other believers, worshiping in the little Burringbar church, and after sunset worship concluded at home, Tom jumped to his feet. "I'm going down to the village."

"What? Are you going to walk four miles in the dark?"

"Yes, I'm going to the post office. I have a hunch that there's a letter there for me, and it has money in it."

Without another word he put on his coat and marched out.

At the foot of the hill trail he heard sulky wheels. David Wyborn, a fellow church member, rolled toward him, also headed in the direction of town. When he saw Tom he pulled his horse up and called out, "Where are you off to at this hour?"

"I'm going to the post office. I have a feeling there's a letter there for me with money in it. Today I put the last money I had into the offering."

David stared down at him. "So did I. I'm in exactly the same situation as you, Tom, 'cept I don't have any hunches about money coming in a letter. Hop in and we'll drive down together."

A few men loitering on the main street of the little town looked up as Dave's clattering sulky shattered the quiet night. Lamplight spilled through the windows of the small post office, and Tom rapped loudly on the pane. Inside he saw the postmaster and his assistant busily sorting mail the carrier had not long ago dumped at the door.

"Is there anything for me, Mr. Masters?" he asked when the postmaster answered his rap.

"I believe there is, Tom." The postmaster adjusted his spectacles and turned back to the huge old desk littered with letters and papers. "Yes, here it is."

Tom took the letter. His trembling, callused finger slit the envelope, and a folded piece of green paper caught his eye. A pound note! Twenty shillings! Exactly twice as much as the offering he had given at church.

"I just thought you might need this," his brother Charlie wrote in the accompanying letter. He had no time for Tom's religion, but he remembered with gratitude the weeks that the younger Crabtree had worked without pay to help him get his farm started.

His feet scarcely touched the ground as Tom strode back to the bakery, where David Wyborn waited for him. "There was! God answered!" Tom bubbled with joy as he told the story. They both bowed their heads and thanked their heavenly Father for His goodness.

"I'm all right. He helped me, too," Dave confided. "The

baker has allowed me credit until my next banana check arrives."

"Wonderful. This is one more evidence of God's love for us."

No one worried too much about trading hours in that little bush community, and Tom hurried around to the back of the baker's shop, where he bought a loaf of bread and a bag of flour. He'd have quite a tale to tell Rosie when he got back home.

History usually repeats itself. Tom's quick, clever move earned him rented land and a firm foothold in the banana-growing community, but, as with Hopping Abe's victory over Squire Broughton, he gained an enemy. After the land-leasing incident Jim Mikks rarely spoke to Tom. In the ensuing years he became more and more bitter and never missed a chance to get even.

Once, when Tom did contract work away from home for several months, the weeds between his long rows of infant bananas grew rank and tall. Jim seized the opportunity to report it to the plantation inspector, who sent a letter threatening that, unless Tom speedily exterminated the weeds, he would take action.

Tom rushed home in response to Rosie's agitated summons. He had to do something quickly, but he could not spare time from the contract work that brought in money so vital to their existence. Nor could be risk his bananas' being condemned and destroyed.

As usual Tom took his problem to God. "What can I do, Lord?" he asked. "I can't take time off to chip out all those weeds. It would take weeks. The boys are too small to do it. Please, show me."

Somewhere Tom had heard of or seen the new knapsack pump sprayers. A man strapped a canful of weed-killing poison on his back and, with the hose and nozzle in his hand, walked up and down between the rows—a fast, sure way to get rid of weeds. But Tom didn't have such a spray and he did not know anyone who did.

Then he remembered a neighbor who had a pump spray that worked on much the same principle. Jubilantly Tom borrowed the heavy can and half-filled it with arsenic solution. Then he set the contraption on the ground and pumped heartily until he built up sufficient air pressure to force the posion out in a fine spray. He had to repeat the performance every ten to fifteen feet, and sweat poured from his brow, but it was faster than hoeing the weeds.

Flushed with that success, Tom wrote to his brothers, David and Charlie, now successful farmers in Victoria, and borrowed £5 to purchase a proper knapsack pump. Other plantation owners noted the speed and efficiency of the knapsack pump and followed his lead—which did not enhance his popularity with Jim Mikks, either. On the slightest pretext he would report Tom and try to cause trouble between him and the authorities.

Then vengeance struck. On one of his routine checks the banana inspector found bunchy-top* in Jim Mikks's plantation.

The very name sent chills of fear into the hearts of banana growers. The mysterious disease spread like wildfire and destroyed a man's hopes overnight. The only way of treating it was to dig up the infected plant, douse it with kerosene, and burn it.

Under the inspector's watchful eyes, Jim dug out and burned stool after stool, row upon row of banana plants. But it was too late. The disease had spread to Tom's plantation.

His heart sank when he first saw the telltale signs: the broken leaf veins, the typical wizened bunching together of the new leaves on the plant's crown. "O God, what will I do?" he groaned aloud.

For the first time in years discouragement shrouded his usual optimism. His shoulders sagged. Slowly he dragged one foot after the other up the steep hill. Each step seemed to drain the energy from his bowed body. He reached the house and told Rosie what he had found.

Her face paled. The dreaded news was not unexpected.

---

* A disease carried by aphids and suspected of originating in the Fijian banana plantations. In the mid-1930s it wiped out whole plantations in Australia.

Everyone knew what had happened to Jim's bananas, and their planation adjoined his. "We can pray," she whispered.

Together they knelt in the kitchen, with the warm sun streaming across the well-scrubbed floorboards and the fowls clucking and pecking in the patch of grass outside the back door. Hand in hand, seeking comfort from each other's presence, they pleaded for the Lord's help.

"There's nothing, absolutely nothing that we can do to stop it from spreading, Lord," Tom prayed. "We put our plantation entirely in Your hands."

Rosie prayed too, reminding Him of their utter dependence upon Him and His mercies.

Suddenly in the midst of her prayer, Tom thought of Malachi 3:10, 11: "Bring ye all the tithes into the storehouse, ... and ... I will ... pour you out a blessing, that there shall not be room enough to receive it. *And I will rebuke the devourer for your sakes,* and he shall not destroy the fruits of your ground."

When his wife finished, he prayed again. Faith surged like fire in his veins, and his voice took on a firm note of assurance. "Dear God, You have promised to rebuke the devourer. We have been faithful with our tithes and offerings, and we claim that promise. Thank You, Lord. Amen."

God, rewarded their faith. As the months passed, Tom had to destroy only one or two plants, and in each case he traced the infection back to Mikks's plantation.

Jim Mikks had not committed his bananas into God's care. No matter what he did he could not arrest the disease in his plants. Eventually he relinquished his lease and left the district.

Tom not only asked God to care for his bananas; he daily placed himself and his family in God's hands. To miss morning worship in the Crabtree household was as unthinkable as missing breakfast. "How can we expect God to supply our daily bread if we neglect our spiritual food?" he asked. And to that question no one could think of a satisfactory answer.

One busy afternoon during the packing season, George, a friend from a nearby plantation, climbed the long hill to the Crabtree door. "Tom," he puffed, "can you lend me your car for a day or two? My wife's mother is staying with us, and she took a bad turn last week. She's not improving much, and my wife thinks we ought to take her in to the hospital."

Mr. Crabtree's ruddy face expressed his concern as he listened to his friend's request. "Of course you can have the old Whippet. That's too bad about your mother-in-law, George. Is there anything else we can do to help?"

"I don't think so, Tom." George took a step toward the gate; then he turned back. "Look, Tom, just in case we're delayed or something; how about if I drive my old 'ute' * over for you to use? I know you have to get your bananas down to the rail, and it would save us both a lot of worry if you had a vehicle."

"Fine, George, that'll be just fine."

They made the swap, and next day Tom and his boys loaded the old utility truck with cases of bananas ready for the city markets. Only as he edged slowly down the steeply graded trail on Weet-Bix Mountain did he discover that the vehicle had no brakes worth mentioning.

"Wow! George should've told me that." Instantly he changed into low gear, and the aged vehicle growled protestingly down the steep slope and out onto the main road.

The remainder of the journey was uneventful. At the railway depot Tom unloaded his cases of bananas and set off for home. All went well until he neared his house on the summit of Weet-Bix Mountain. Yelling and waving their welcome to their father, Lindsay and Barry ran out to open the plantation's double gates. Then it happened.

The ancient engine stalled. Frantically Tom pumped on the useless brakes—nothing happened. The truck started to carren backward down the trail, and before he could leap to safety, it reached the edge of the hill and plunged over.

The first roll smashed the cab's wooden ribs, and the fabric roof collapsed onto Tom's head, enveloping him in its smothering folds. Unable to free himself from the hampering cloth, he had no hope of jumping out of the truck. Desperately he clung to the steering column, the only stable item in the madly tumbling vehicle. The utility somersaulted over and

---

* Utility vehicle, akin to an American pickup truck.

over, each landing cushioned by the profuse growth of lantana bushes.

"God help me! God save . . . save me!" There was no time for pleading and claiming promises. His body, jammed in between the seat and the steering column, jerked and rolled with each movement of the truck. "Help, God!" Finally the vehicle hit a fallen log, slithered the last fifty yards to the bottom of the mountain, and settled, wheels in air, at the base of a mighty eucalyptus tree.

In the silence that followed, Tom clearly heard far above him his boys crying, "Mother, Mother! Dad's gone over the edge. He's killed! Oh, Mother, Mother!"

Dizzy and shaken, he fought himself free of the tangled mass of splintered wood and tattered canvas and crawled out of the battered vehicle just as Rosie and his sons slipped and slid down the mountain toward him.

Lindsay saw him first. "There's Dad! He's alive!" He pointed a shaking finger toward the pile of broken bushes. In a moment they reached his side. "Are you hurt? Dad, are you all right?"

White as a ghost and shivering with shock, Tom said huskily, "Yes, I'm all right. God saved me."

"You're not all right. You're injured." His wife tore at his bloodsoaked shirt where the shattered steering wheel had pierced his chest. Tears rained down her cheeks when she found that the wound was superficial.

"Thank God! Oh, thank God!"

Gingerly he stamped his feet and flexed his arms. No bones broken. With Rosie and the boys on either side to lend support, he half-crawled back up the hill, staggered across the road, and collapsed gratefully onto a chair in the humble little home that he had never expected to enter again.

While the boys watched sympathetically, Rosie cleaned the jagged wound and dabbed it liberally with iodine. Tom grimaced and groaned as she bandaged his chest, but the next day found him back in the shed packing bananas.

A borrowed cart and Nugget, the faithful old draft horse,

solved the problem of taking the bananas to the railway, but getting the utility truck up the hill was a different matter.

Today's affluence and comprehensive insurance policies would probably have classified it as a write-off, and it would be left to rust at the foot of the tree. But few people living in Burringbar then could afford insurance, and fewer still considered a vehicle, no matter how old and battered it might be, beyond salvage.

With the help of a block and tackle and many neighborly hands, Tom hauled the utility from its resting place among the ferns and lantana. To everyone's surprise the sturdy old vehicle's engine started up at the first try, and, apart from a few extra scratches and a dented fender, the bodywork looked little the worse for catapulting down the mountainside.

"She'll need a new roof, Tom, and a steerin' wheel. An this front headlamp needs straightenin'. I reckon fifteen pounds'll cover the lot."

The neighbor was correct. For £15 Tom had the utility repaired, including new brake linings, and handed it back to George a few weeks later. Of course, he told his friend what had happened, and together they pushed their way downhill through the crushed lantana bushes, following the vehicle's progress down the mountain.

"Y' musta rolled at least twelve times, Tom. Y' can see the marks each time it landed wheels down and rolled again. It's a miracle y're alive."

"It is a miracle," he agreed fervently, and quoted " 'Then they cried unto the Lord in their trouble, and he saved them out of their distresses. He brought them out of darkness and the shadow of death, and brake their bands in sunder. Oh that men would praise the Lord for his goodness, and for his wonderful works to the children of men!' * I cried unto the Lord, George, and He saved me, and I'll praise and thank Him all the days of my life."

The runaway-truck incident was not the only time that Tom escaped death in the hills around Burringbar. On another memorable occasion he was working alone felling trees and

* Ps. 107:13-15.

clearing scrub in readiness for planting banana suckers. One of the trees, a huge dead gum lifting leafless branches high into the air, looked dry enough to burn.

I reckon I'll save time and trouble and burn this old fellow, Tom thought to himself, squinting up at the fretwork of limbs, ghostly gray against the azure sky. It looked old and was probably rotted inside. It shouldn't take too long to burn.

Working quickly, he piled a heap of dried leaves and branches from other trees around the giant's base and set them afire. Then he put the matches in his pocket and stepped back to watch.

Suddenly a faint, creaking groan made him look up. The top of the tall tree seemed to sway toward him. Petrified with fear, Tom stood for a few seconds unable to believe his eyes. Was it coming down so soon? A louder creak, and another. He had no doubt in his mind now.

"Lord, save me!" he cried in terror.

To run right or left uphill was impossible. Those spreading branches spelled doom. His only hope lay in racing down the mountainside ahead of the falling tree.

In the split second it took to make that decision, his legs flew into action. Like a puppet propelled by an unseen power, he cleared rocks and fallen logs in great flying leaps. His heart pounded, his breath whistled through clenched teeth.

"God, save me!"

Tom's legs worked like pistons. He couldn't have stopped his mad bounding if he had wanted to. Behind, he heard the cracking, rushing sound gaining on him. "Help, God! Help!"

The rushing grew to a roar. His clothes flapped wildly in the gusts generated by the falling giant. A crash like a mighty thunderclap reverberated in his ears and a rain of snapped twigs pelted his trembling body.

Suddenly his feet shot from under him and he landed flat on his back and rolled sideways, only inches from the exploding branches.

When silence settled over the bush Tom shakily rose to his knees. "Thank You, God." He raised his eyes to the cloudless blue sky above. Then he looked down at the litter of twisted, splintered branches lying all around him. "Thank You for saving me from a horrible death."

On other occasions too numerous to mention Tom saw miracles in Marmite* Valley.

Venomous snakes abounded in the dense scrub. Sometimes a man would shoulder a heavy stalk of bananas uphill to the packing shed and discover, when he took his large curved knife to cut off the "hands" of fruit, a poisonous reptile curled around the stalk. A "flying fox," the taut wire used for hauling goods up and down the steep mountains, sometimes snapped. The recoil could sever a man's limb if he was in the way.

But land clearing was the most dangerous occupation. Frequent felling accidents, or near accidents, kept Tom and his neighbors alert to the uncertainty of life—particularly one lived without thought of God.

Tom had another narrow escape when he and some neighbors tried to fell a mighty tree. Bill and Tom stood on springboards,† chopping away on either side of the giant trunk. Suddenly they heard a rending crash, and the huge tree, dragged down by the weight of its own leaves and branches, split about ten feet up from where they balanced.

"Jump for it, Tom!" Bill shouted and leaped to safety. But Tom, chopping on the opposite side, was too late. He clung to the half-severed trunk praying desperately while the forest giant creaked and groaned and rocked.

Once again God heard his prayer. With a terrifying, smashing crash, the top of the great tree splintered off, swishing right over Tom's head on its way to the ground.

Unlike his grandfather, Abe, Tom was not acquainted with the inside of a courtroom. He had never knowingly broken the laws of the land and had no intention of doing so. But one time he let his Lord down badly and found himself standing before a judge. Forty years later he still hangs his head in shame at recollection of it.

Like most mountains of evil it began with a molehill. Tom's

---

* Marmite and Weet-Bix are two of the well-known health foods manufactured in Australia by the Seventh-day-Adventist-owned Sanitarium Health Food Company.

oldest son forgot to close a common gate that the Crabtrees shared with a neighbor who grazed cattle on his land. No harm was done, but the furious man rode over to Tom's place and blamed him for negligence.

One word led to another, and finally the neighbor lost all control and swore at Tom. He hurled foul insults at the top of his voice until Tom said evenly, "Be quiet, Mr. Shell. Someday someone will punch your nose for using language like that."

"Oh, will they?" the enraged man shrieked. He flung his bridle to the ground and clenched his fists. "Come on then, you cowardly so and so. Come and do it."

At that instant Abe's fierce temper bridged the generation gap. Tom saw red. As the infuriated man lunged toward him, Tom's jaw-centered punch sent Shell reeling to the ground.

Within days he had a summons to court to answer a charge of assault. But the judge postponed the case because one of the lawyers was ill, and that gave Tom more time to cool down. He thought things over and realized that, no matter how severe the provocation or how righteous the cause, he had not acted in a Christian manner.

But it took much prayer and many days of battling against his pride before he could go down to the neighbor's house and apologize. Even that did not satisfy the spiteful man. Nothing would suffice but that Tom present a written apology that he could flaunt in front of his friends.

It was hard to do. His face flamed and the nails of his clenched fists furrowed the palms of his hands. But with a silent prayer for help, he sat down at the neighbor's table and wrote:

"Inasmuch as I wish to have a conscience void of offense toward God and man, I herewith state that I am sorry that I hit one man, namely Mr. Shell, and I now ask Mr. Shell to forgive me. Signed, Thomas Crabtree."

Then Tom handed the paper over and they shook hands. Also Tom agreed to pay all the court costs involved in the case, and there the matter ended. Or did it?

The whole district buzzed over the affair. Even Crabtree's

worst critics agreed that, despite his lapse, he had acted like a Christian when making amends.

Eight years passed. With the fruiting of his bananas, Tom's fortunes changed. He still toiled from dawn to dusk and did the work of two men, but as the boys grew they helped him. The family had to cut heavy bunches of green fruit and carry them on their backs up the hill to the packing shed. The wood for the fruit cases came ready-cut, but each case they had to nail together and arrange the hands of unripe bananas just so. Many a time Rosie left her housework and stood in the drafty, rickety shed and helped to sort and pack bananas, hundreds of thousands of them.

Gradually Tom and Rosie paid off their debts, educated their children, purchased a secondhand 1927 Whippet car, and built a new house. But always Tom's foremost interest was to witness for his Lord.

Everyone in Burringbar and the surrounding district knew the Adventists, particularly Tom Crabtree from Marmite Valley. He was the first "feller who keeps Saturday fer Sunday," that they had ever seen. Everywhere he went people eyed him, wondering what kind of strange creature he was. They heard about his dietary habits, too, and scornfully said, "Oh, here's that feller from Weet-Bix Mountain who's turned the district upside down."

His reputation pleased Tom. "That's what they said about the apostle Paul," he reminded Rosie.

He and most of the other Seventh-day Adventist believers of that era carried out Mrs. E. G. White's injunction to "scatter tracts like the leaves of autumn," except that they didn't scatter them. They delivered them personally. From house to house, farm to farm, up and down the hills and valleys they went.

One afternoon Tom called at a house about 4:00 P.M. and found the whole family down at the dairy milking the cows. "Good afternoon," he yelled cheerfully above the clatter of pails and hoofs and the soft swish-swish of milk jets streaming into frothing buckets. "I've brought you something to read when the work is done."

The two teen-age sons, busy driving the cows into the bails,* exchanged glances but said nothing. The woman, milking a cow just inside the bails, raised her head and nodded a brief acknowledgment of Tom's presence.

But the man whirled around as if he had been stung. "We don't want yer books," he snarled and raised his heavy steel milk bucket threateningly. "Get outa here afore I knock yer down."

His wife leaped up and grabbed his arm. Apologetically she explained, "We're all strict Church of England Christians here."

Smiling, Tom raised his hat. "Thank you for telling me. I've never before known a Church of England Christian, or any other kind, to threaten another Christian with a milk bucket."

One of his regular calls was to the sisters at the Roman Catholic convent, who purchased *Uncle Arthur's Bedtime Stories* from him. He often picked them up in his car when he saw them trudging along the road, perspiring in their heavy black habits. Usually he met them when he and his family were on the way home from church and the sisters were off to visit some of their sick members. Then Tom's boys alighted and ran along the road to catch up later with the car, and the sisters took their places and thankfully rode the short distance to the Mills house.

Mr. and Mrs. Mills, the two nuns, and Tom became good friends. The four Roman Catholics appreciated his kindness so much that they did their level best to convert him. Many times they tried to reason with him and point out the "errors" in his theology, but for every argument Tom had a text to prove his point.

"Oh, dear me, you know your Bible so well," Sister Therese fluttered. "If only you knew the traditions of the Catholic Church, you'd make a wonderful Catholic. It's such a pity."

"But, sister," Tom protested earnestly, "I *do* know the traditions of the Roman Catholic Church, and that is *why* I am a Seventh-day Adventist."

Jack was a World War I veteran who lived with his sister and

---

* Frames for confining the heads of the cows.

her husband on a plantation four miles out of Burringbar. During his first year in the valley Tom worked alongside him and learned how to grade and pack bananas. All the while they labored together Tom witnessed to the old fellow, but he proved unresponsive. "I'm a bit of a loner, Tom, and I love a drink," he excused himself. "Religion ain't fer the likes of me."

One Saturday afternoon Jack went into the little township and drank so much that he caused a disturbance in the street. The hastily summoned local policeman tried to reason with him. "Now look here, Jack, you'd better——"

"Don' you—hic—touch me." Jack swayed toward the policeman and clenched his fists. "I'll—hic—show you a thing or two."

"Aw, go along home, Jack. Don't fall foul of the law." The policeman took him by the shoulders and gave him a push in the right direction.

By the time Jack staggered four miles home he was stone sober, and when he learned what a spectacle he had made of himself, he swore off drinking for good.

Many months later he came to Tom's door and asked for work. A little questioning revealed that his sister and brother-in-law had kicked him out because, in a bitter family argument relating to religion, Jack had stood up for the Seventh-day Adventists.

"All right. You can help me pack bananas."

Tom lent Jack a tent to live in and paid him a daily wage for his work. But the arragement did not last long. Early one morning, while the Crabtree family was still at breakfast, he staggered up to the back door.

"Tom," he groaned, "can you take me in ter the docter? I gotta dreadful pain in me insides."

The "dreadful pain" proved to be cancer. The doctors operated on him, but his case was beyond medical help, and he was transferred to Brisbane city hospital. As soon as he could, Tom drove up to visit him.

After they had discussed general topics for a little while, the dying man said, "Aw, Tom, you used to talk to me about God, but I didn't listen properly. Now it's too late. I've got cancer. I'm going to croak."

"No, Jack. No, it's not too late. God loves you. He is waiting to forgive your sins and accept you as His humble child. Now, Jack, tell Him that you love Him, right now."

Tears came into the old man's pain-racked eyes, and he grasped Tom's hand in an iron grip. "I will, Tom, I will."

Jack made his peace with God, and not long afterward he slipped into unconsciousness.

One afternoon Tom and some of the other Adventist men from the valley drove down to Mullumbimby to sell small religious books and distribute *Signs of the Times.* Never one to pass a door, Tom walked into the bar of the Central Hotel. For a few moments he stood disgustedly sniffing the mingled odors of beer and tobacco smoke. Then someone noticed him and yelled above the buzz of voices and clink of glasses, "What d'ya want in here, mate?"

"I want you," Tom replied. "I want to give you something to read." Then he walked across to the man and held out *Signs.* The man put down his beer mug and took the magazine. Others crowded around Tom. Here was something for nothing! Tom put a *Signs* into each clutching hand. Some of them read the cover and tossed him a penny in payment; others stuffed the periodical inside their shirts and went back to their beer.

Tom turned toward the door, and the proprietor, standing behind the bar with his hand on the beer pump, called after him, "Will you have a taste?"

"No, thank you, but I appreciate your hospitality." He passed the proprietor a *Signs,* waved a cheery goodbye to the men, and went on his way.

More than a year later Tom visited the Seventh-day Adventist sanitarium in Sydney. During his short stay there a woman spoke to him. "I see that you Seventh-day Adventists are building a church in Mullumbimby," she said conversationally.

"That's correct." He wondered who the woman was and

how she knew about the church.

Seeing his puzzled expression, she laughed and explained, "I'm Mrs. McDougall from the Central Hotel in Mullumbimby."

His eyebrows shot up. "That's a long way from Sydney. How did you come to know about this hospital?"

"Oh, I read about it in the *Signs of the Times* that you gave to my husband. It sounded like a fine hospital, so I decided to come down here. I'm so glad I did. I love the place, and the nurses and doctors are so kind and attentive. I think it must be their religion."

"Oh, it is, it is," he assured her.

Among the many people whom Tom led to Christ in the Burringbar district were a considerable number that he did not know about until years later. Once, when he was an old man, a woman introduced herself to him at camp meeting. "You won't remember me," she said, "but as a little girl I lived in Burringbar. Every Saturday I used to stand at our front gate and watch the carloads of Adventists going by on their way to church. You all looked so happy. I wished that I could go too. When I grew up and married, both my husband and I eventually became Seventh-day Adventists."

An old man who joined the church some time after Tom had left Burringbar said, "On Friday nights we heard your family singing hymns. The sound echoed all over the quiet hills and valleys. I used to sit out on my front steps and listen, and I'd weep. I'd weep because I didn't have what you people had.

"That was a long while ago, and times have changed. The little old church has gone—sold to a farmer who uses it as a barn. Everyone owns cars now. Prosperity has come to the valley, and the Seventh-day Adventists living there now go away on Sabbaths. They drive off to attend the big churches in Mullumbimby and Murwillumbah and Lismore."

In 1940 the conference president visited the Adventists around Burringbar and spent a long time talking to Tom. The fiery impetuosity he had inherited from his grandfather Abe, now tempered by the Spirit of God, resulted in his being a fearless witness for the Seventh-day Adventist Church, and the local conference president recognized that fact.

"You've done a great work here in Burringbar, Tom, but now there are plenty of others who can carry it on. We need someone like you and Brother Chilcott to settle in Mullumbimby and spread the message there. What would you think about that?"

He did not reply, so the church official continued. "Pastor Llewellyn Jones held an evangelistic series there, and Charlie Parmenter has canvassed in that territory. We have about a dozen church members, but the work needs building up."

Still Tom said nothing. He had been to Mullumbimby distributing tracts and booklets, even giving Bible studies, and had met with meager response. As a result he did not share the president's enthusiasm for the plan.

"It's good banana country. If you and Brother Chilcott moved down there, you could . . ."

Tom was not happy with the suggestion. After living for eight years in the banana house, as they called it, he had recently completed a new home for his wife. A *real* house, the finest they had ever lived in. Their bananas were doing well, too. Life was easier than it had ever been for Tom. They had a thriving church, and Percy Steer had promised to donate land for a church school. Why should he leave all their friends and go to a new place to begin all over again?

Besides, World War II was gaining momentum, putting men and materials in short supply. He would not be able to build Rosie another house. It wasn't fair to her—what with the new baby expected any day.

Nevertheless Tom yielded to the conference president's pleas to "go and have a look at the prospects." On the twenty-ninth of October, with his three sons, Lindsay, Barry, and David, he drove to the Main Arm district of the Brunswick River—and promptly fell in love with the place.

Nowhere else had he seen such soil, so many gently sloping hills. "This is perfect banana-growing country," he crowed to the boys, and they agreed. Before the day ended he signed up for the place adjoining the Chilcotts and Parmenters, Seventh-day Adventist families already living there.

When they arrived back at Burringbar a man waited at their front gate. "Mr. Crabtree," he said when Tom alighted from the car and asked his business, "I'd like to settle in this district. Are you wanting to sell your house and farm?"

Tom stared at him dumbfounded. Surely the Lord must want him to move to Mullumbimby.

On the same day that Tom and the boys visited Mullumbimby, Rosie went to the hospital for the birth of their second daughter. Her husband rushed in to see her that night, duly admired the new baby, and then dropped his bombshell. "We're moving to Mulumbimby. God wants us there. The president was right."

Within a week it was all settled. He sold the house and farm, and the family moved to Main Arm, onto ten acres of banana-bearing plantation and another ten acres of uncleared land.

And then everything went wrong, and Tom began to have second thoughts. Lindsay, their eldest son, came down with pneumonia and almost lost his life. While helping to chop down a tree, Barry's ax fouled with an overhanging vine and almost severed his foot. Tom's own heart almost failed when he looked about at the vast expanse of uncleared land with its trees to fell, thick scrub to brush-hook down, dry, and burn, and the heavy, root-matted earth to dig and loosen. Why was he starting again from scratch at his age? Surely he had acted too rashly?

They faced enmity, from the neighbors. "How come?" they asked, "that these Adventist young men are not joining the Forces and going off to war? Why should they be at home making money when our sons are fighting and dying for their country?"

The Crabtrees had no house to live in. Not even a shack. They lived in a tent while Rosie cooked camp style and did the family wash in water carted up from the creek. But if she ever shed a tear for the comfortable new house that she had enjoyed so briefly, no one knew about it. With the same radiant

Christianity, the same faith in God's leading that had sustained her for nearly two decades, she stood uncomplainingly by her husband's side.

Ultimately their situation improved. The bananas bore fruit. "But not as good as those we had in Burringbar," Tom commented ruefully. A house and garden took shape. Barry went off to college and became a minister. The other children grew and prospered and became pillars in their church and community.

Then one fine day Tom's parents came to visit. Old David Crabtree was full of praise when he saw how Tom had carved a home and a comfortable living out of the subtropical wilderness. As the days passed, his admiration for his third son grew, and finally he brokenly asked pardon for the harsh treatment he had meted out so many years ago.

"Of course. Of course I forgive you." Tom hugged his father. "Don't ever think of it again."

From Tom's place the old couple journeyed across to Inverell to spend some time with Gladys, Tom's twin sister, who had married and settled in that district. "What is it that has made Tom so different?" David asked her one day. "He was such a wild young fellow—swearing, smoking, drinking. Now he doesn't do anything like that. He doesn't even eat meat or drink tea."

"It's because of his religion," she explained. "The Bible says that our bodies are temples of the Holy Ghost and we should keep them clean and holy."

"The Bible says that, does it?" Her father thoughtfully tapped his old pipe, constant companion of many years, on the palm of his hand. "Well, if Tom can do it, so can I." While his wife and daughter watched in speechless amazement, the old man took his worn tobacco pouch out of his pocket, lifted the lid of the kitchen stove, and threw both articles into the flames.

Some time later Tom had another visit from his parents. Damaris spent most of her time in the house with Rosie and the grandchildren, but Tom and his father tramped up and down the hill, cutting and carting bananas. While they worked they talked of many things, including religion.

"Of course I believe in Jesus," the old man assured Tom. "I pray to God three times every day."

He never joined the Seventh-day Adventist Church, and not long after his confession of faith, Tom stood beside his deathbed. For many hours the old man had lain in a coma. Suddenly he roused, looked up at Tom, and with great effort clasped his thin, gnarled hands in an attitude of prayer. While Tom and the other relatives watched through tear-misted eyes, he quietly sank into the sleep from which only Jesus can awaken him.

Gladys, Tom's twin sister, had long ago followed his example and devoted her life to God's cause. They both prayed earnestly for the rest of the family, but only Damaris joined them. Always a God-fearing woman, it took a long time for her to recognize that faith and obedience walk hand in hand. Finally, at the age of 87, she chose to be baptized into the Seventh-day Adventist Church.

David, Tom's closest brother, stubbornly resisted his pleas that he surrender his life to God. "Aw, cut it out," he protested whenever the matter came up. "I've got no time for psalm singers. I'll take my chance when the time comes."

"But you have no chance, no chance at all, without Christ in your heart," Tom pleaded. But he, like the others, died without God.

Just as surely as old Hopping Abe had faithful friends, as well as bitter enemies, so his grandson Tom engendered both hate and good will in his tireless efforts to proclaim God's truth. For more than forty-five years he moved from place to place witnessing for his Lord. During that time he watched his children, grandchildren, and now great-grandchildren grow up to follow his example and look forward to the coming of their Saviour.

Tom is still actively working to spread the gospel message. One of his greatest joys is when strangers—or friends from long ago—come up, shake his hand, and say:

"You won't remember me, Mr. Crabtree, but you helped me to find Christ when we lived in Mullumbimby."

"Years and years ago when you gave a *Signs of the Times* to my mother. Well, I'm here in church as a result of that contact."

"You never knew it, Tom, but your witness led me and my family to the truth . . ."

---

† A short board inserted in a notch on the tree trunk. The axman stands on it to chop on the tree.